Methods of Analysis and Detection

Anne McCarthy

Series editor: Brian Ratcliff

CAMBRIDGE
UNIVERSITY PRESS

PUBLISHED BY THE PRESS SYNDICATE OF THE UNIVERSITY OF CAMBRIDGE
The Pitt Building, Trumpington Street, Cambridge, United Kingdom

CAMBRIDGE UNIVERSITY PRESS
The Edinburgh Building, Cambridge CB2 2RU, UK
40 West 20th Street, New York, NY 10011–4211, USA
10 Stamford Road, Oakleigh, VIC 3166, Australia
Ruiz de Alarcón 13, 28014 Madrid, Spain
Dock House, The Waterfront, Cape Town 8001, South Africa

http://www.cambridge.org

First published 2001

Printed in the United Kingdom at the University Press, Cambridge

Typeface Swift   *System* QuarkXPress®

A catalogue record for this book is available from the British Library

ISBN 0 521 78724 6 paperback

Produced by Gecko Ltd, Bicester, Oxon

Front cover photographs: Scanning tunnelling micrograph of gold atoms
(shown here as yellow, red and brown) on graphite substrate (shown green);
Phillipe Plailly/Science Photo Library

Contents

Introduction

Cambridge Advanced Sciences

The *Cambridge Advanced Sciences* series has been developed to meet the demands of all the new AS and A level science examinations. In particular, it has been endorsed by OCR as providing complete coverage of their specifications. The AS material is presented as a single text for each of biology, chemistry and physics. Material for the A2 year comprises six books in each subject: one of core material and one for each option. Some material has been drawn from the existing *Cambridge Modular Sciences* books; however, the majority is entirely new.

During the development of this series, the opportunity has been taken to improve the design, and a complete and thorough new writing and editing process has been applied. Much more material is now presented in colour. Although the existing *Cambridge Modular Sciences* texts do cover some of the new specifications, the *Cambridge Advanced Sciences* books cover every OCR learning objective in detail. They are the key to success in the new AS and A level examinations.

OCR is one of the three unitary awarding bodies offering the full range of academic and vocational qualifications in the UK. For full details of the new specifications, please contact OCR:

OCR, 1 Hills Rd, Cambridge CB1 2EU
Tel: 01223 553311   http://www.ocr.org.uk

The presentation of units

You will find that the books in this series use a bracketed convention in the presentation of units within tables and on graph axes. For example, ionisation energies of $1000 \, kJ \, mol^{-1}$ and $2000 \, kJ \, mol^{-1}$ will be represented in this way:

Measurement	Ionisation energy ($kJ \, mol^{-1}$)
1	1000
2	2000

OCR examination papers use the solidus as a convention, thus:

Measurement	Ionisation energy / $kJ \, mol^{-1}$
1	1000
2	2000

Any numbers appearing in brackets with the units, for example ($10^{-5} \, mol \, dm^{-3} \, s^{-1}$), should be treated in exactly the same way as when preceded by the solidus, /$10^{-5} \, mol \, dm^{-3} \, s^{-1}$.

Methods of Analysis and Detection – an A2 option text

Methods of Analysis and Detection contains everything needed to cover the A2 option of the same name. It combines entirely new text and illustrations with revised and updated material from the first edition of *Methods of Analysis and Detection*, previously available in the *Cambridge Modular Sciences* series.

The book is divided into five chapters corresponding to the modules Separation Techniques for Analysis, Mass Spectrometry, Atomic Emission Spectroscopy, Ultraviolet/Visible Absorption Spectroscopy, and Combined Techniques.

In addition, a specialised glossary of terms is included, linked to the main text via the index. Please note that some prior knowledge required to study this option is not covered until the synoptic unit of the A2 course. However, supporting material can be found in *Chemistry 2*.

Acknowledgements

1.14, Action Plus; 1.15, copyright © BBC (BBC News and Current Affairs Stills Picture Library); 1.18, 1.24, Cellmark Diagnostics; 1.25, 2.4a, Robert Harding Picture Library; 1.26, courtesy of Helen Parkes/LGC, Teddington; 2.1a, 3.11a, 3.11b, Mary Evans Picture Library; 2.1b, Science and Society Picture Library; 2.11, E.T. Archive; 3.3a, 3.3b, Courtauld Institute; 3.12c, Geoff Tompkinson/ Science Photo Library; 3.13, Ann Ronan at Image Select International; 3.15, courtesy of Addenbrookes Hospital Medical Photography Unit

Picture research: Maureen Cowdroy

CHAPTER 1

Separation techniques for analysis

By the end of this chapter you should be able to:

1 describe simply and explain qualitatively the following: paper, thin-layer and gas/liquid chromatography in terms of partition and adsorption;

2 explain the terms R_f value and retention time;

3 interpret one-way and two-way chromatograms in terms of the identification of a particular component of a mixture;

4 interpret gas/liquid chromatograms in terms of the percentage composition of a mixture;

5 describe simply the process of electrophoresis;

6 describe the separation and detection of amino acids by electrophoresis, including the use of changing the pH;

7 outline the extraction of DNA, the separation of the genetic fragments by electrophoresis and their detection using phosphorus-32 to produce a genetic fingerprint (DNA profile).

Chromatography and electrophoresis are both methods of analysis that separate substances, but the principles involved in each are quite different.

Chromatography

You may remember with pride, in primary or lower-school science, splitting up the components of ink from fibre-tip pens or separating the colours of Smarties on filter paper (*figure 1.1*). This type of simple experiment has been developed, so that we can now separate many different kinds of substances.

The separation of substances by their slow movement through or over a separating material is called **chromatography**. The word 'chromatography', which means 'colour writing', was first used in 1903 to describe the separation of plant

pigments by percolating a solution of the plant pigments through a column of calcium carbonate packed into a glass tube (*figure 1.2*). Different pigments moved at different rates and formed different coloured areas in the column, and so could be separated. Although many of the substances that we now separate by the more

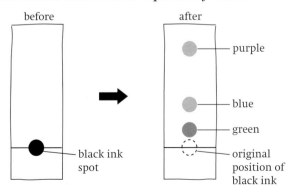

● **Figure 1.1** Separating the components of black ink from a fibre-tip pen. Chromatography shows that the black ink is a mixture of three different colours.

recent, more developed methods are colourless, we still use the term chromatography.

You can see in *figure 1.2* how the solution of pigments is placed on top of the column and is washed down the column with a solvent. This simple process, and the more advanced methods of chromatography, all have the following principles in common.

- There are two phases in the chromatography process – the **stationary phase** and the **mobile phase**. (i) The stationary phase stays in place inside the column or in the fibres of the paper. If the stationary phase is packed into a column it usually consists of solid particles or a viscous liquid coated onto a solid surface. (ii) The mobile phase, which is the **solvent**, moves through the column or over the paper and is either a liquid or a gas.
- The separation of the mixture we want to study occurs because the components of the mixture interact with the stationary phase to differing extents.
- Dissolved components are called **solutes**.
- There are two mechanisms for the separation process: (i) partition and (ii) adsorption.

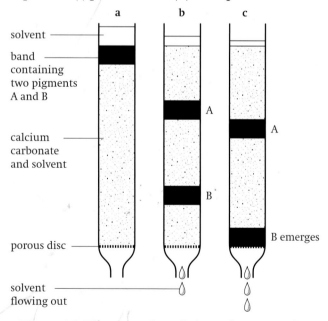

- **Figure 1.2** The separation of plant pigments – the first example of chromatography.
- **a** The mixed pigments are added to the top of a column of $CaCO_3$.
- **b** The pigments flow downwards with the solvent, but at different rates.
- **c** The pigments reach the bottom of the column at different times and can be collected separately.

Mechanisms of chromatographic separation

Partition

To understand the term **partition**, it is helpful to examine what happens to a solute when it is added to two liquids that do not mix but which are in contact with one another. For example, when bromine is added to a mixture of water and tribromomethane ($CHBr_3$), two liquid layers form and the bromine molecules pass upwards and downwards across the interface between the liquids (*figure 1.3*). When the rates of movement of the solute molecules up and down between the two liquids become equal, we say that *equilibrium* has been reached. At equilibrium the solute molecules are distributed between the two liquids in a definite ratio; the solute has been partitioned between the two liquids. (For more information about equilibria, see *Chemistry 1* chapter 15.)

During the separation process in partition chromatography, the solutes move between the stationary phase and the mobile phase (*figure 1.4a*) and are partitioned between them. Solutes in the mobile phase move forward with it.

When the stationary and mobile phases are both liquids, the rate of movement of each solute depends on its *relative solubility* in the two phases. Solutes that are more soluble in the mobile phase will move faster than the others and will either move further or leave the column earlier. When the mobile phase is a gas, the rate of movement of the solutes depends on their *volatility* and their *relative solubility*.

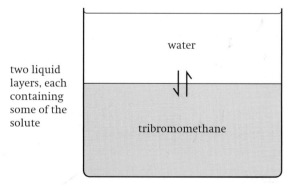

- **Figure 1.3** Bromine partitioned between water and tribromomethane.

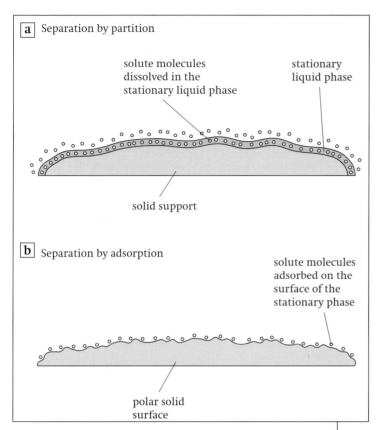

a Separation by partition

solute molecules dissolved in the stationary liquid phase

stationary liquid phase

solid support

b Separation by adsorption

solute molecules adsorbed on the surface of the stationary phase

polar solid surface

● **Figure 1.4** The two mechanisms of separation:
a partition chromatography;
b adsorption chromatography.

Adsorption

In **adsorption chromatography**, the solute molecules are held on the surface of the stationary phase (*figure 1.4b*). The stationary phase is a polar solid and the solutes are polar molecules. Strongly polar stationary phases attract and retain the polar solutes. The separation of the solutes depends on the *difference in their polarity*; the more polar solutes are more readily adsorbed than the less polar solutes. (For more information about polarity see *Chemistry 1*, chapter 3.)

Paper chromatography

In paper chromatography filter paper is used because the cellulose fibres from which it is made contain water. This trapped water is the stationary phase and the filter paper is called the **support**. The mobile phase is the liquid solvent that moves over the paper.

Figure 1.5a shows how the method works. The solutes are transferred from the mobile phase to the stationary phase by partition between the two liquids. Solutes in the mobile phase move forward with it.

When the solvent comes towards the top of the paper, the paper is removed from the chromatography tank and the solvent is allowed to evaporate. Coloured components of a mixture can be seen directly. When colourless components are involved, you can spray the paper with chemicals so that the colourless components form coloured complex ions. For example, when sprayed with ninhydrin, amino acids show up as lilac-blue spots.

Figure 1.5b shows how the components of the mixture are identified by comparing their positions on the filter paper with those of known pure compounds.

Another way to identify the components of a mixture is to calculate their retardation factors

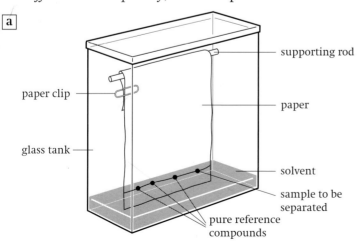

a

supporting rod

paper clip

paper

glass tank

solvent

sample to be separated

pure reference compounds

b

solvent front

pure reference compounds

mixture of solutes to be identified

● **Figure 1.5**
a One-way paper chromatography.
b Components of the unknown mixture can be identified by comparison with pure reference compounds.

(R_f values). The movement of any solute relative to the solvent is a characteristic property of the solute. The R_f value is defined as:

$$R_f = \frac{\text{distance moved by centre of solute spot}}{\text{distance moved by front of mobile phase}}$$

The method for calculating an R_f value is shown in *figure 1.6*.

You may have wondered what we can do if the solvent does not completely separate two or more of the components. This difficulty can be overcome by rotating the paper through 90° after the initial process and repeating the separation with a different solvent, as shown in *figure 1.7*. Separation of all the components should now occur, as it is unlikely that two or more substances would have identical R_f values in two different solvents. This technique is known as **two-way chromatography**.

Paper chromatography is a sensitive method, capable of separating samples as small as 0.1 μg (1 μg = 1 × 10^{-6} g).

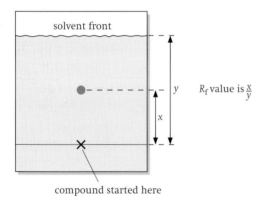

● **Figure 1.6** Calculation of R_f values.

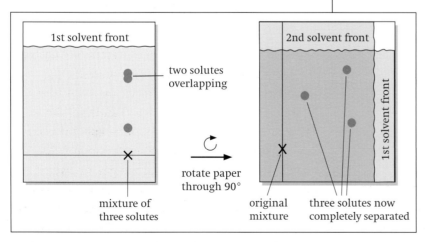

● **Figure 1.7** Two-way paper chromatography.

Thin-layer chromatography

In thin-layer chromatography (TLC), the stationary phase is a thin layer of silica (SiO_2) or aluminium oxide (Al_2O_3), which is coated onto a glass or plastic surface. The mobile phase is a liquid (*figure 1.8*).

The silica or aluminium oxide is first heated to a high temperature so that all water is removed from it. In this state these compounds act as polar solids and the solutes are transferred to them from the mobile phase by adsorption onto their surfaces. However, both these stationary phases readily attract water molecules, so that the thin layers become $SiO_2.xH_2O$ (silica gel) or $Al_2O_3.xH_2O$ (alumina). The water present then becomes the stationary phase and the solutes are separated by partition. On partially dried thin layers, both adsorption and partition may occur.

A thin layer of cellulose powder can also be used as the stationary phase, but, as the cellulose retains water, the separation is by partition.

Colourless components can be detected by the use of appropriate chemicals. One procedure is to place the plate in a closed container with a few crystals of iodine. The iodine vapour accumulates on the spots of separated solutes, so that dark-brown spots appear on a yellow background. For example, the products resulting from the nitration of phenol (2-nitrophenol and 4-nitrophenol) may be separated and located in this way.

A second technique involves shining ultraviolet light onto a plate that contains a fluorescent material. The glow is reduced by the solutes, which will then appear as dark spots on a bright plate. The solutes are identified in the same way as for paper chromatography, using R_f values and pure reference compounds.

Thin-layer chromatography is about three times as fast as paper chromatography and it will work with very small samples. You may be able to try it yourself using a coated microscope slide. Also, because the thin layer can be made from different solids, a wide range of mixtures can be separated and the components of the mixtures identified by careful choice of both

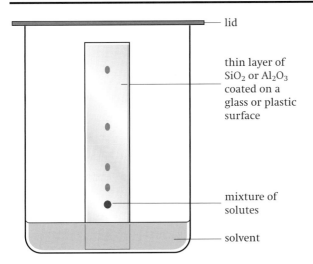

● **Figure 1.8** Thin-layer chromatography.

the stationary and mobile phases. For example, a thin layer of silica will separate chlorinated insecticides, steroids or alkaloids such as morphine and opium.

Thin-layer chromatography can also be used to select the conditions for larger-scale separations. Different combinations of stationary phases and mobile phases can be tested quickly to find the most effective method for a particular separation.

Thin-layer chromatography is mainly used for the separation of organic compounds and has applications in clinical diagnosis, forensic testing and quality control.

SAQ 1.1

State two advantages of thin-layer chromatography over paper chromatography.

SAQ 1.2

The results of a thin-layer chromatography separation on silica gel are shown below.

Compound	Distance travelled (cm)
compound 1	1.5
compound 2	9.1
solvent	12.5

Calculate the R_f values of the compounds and comment on their values.
Hint: consider the nature of the thin layer.

Examples of the use of thin-layer chromatography in forensic science are the well publicised cases of the 'Maguire Seven' and the 'Birmingham Six',

men and women suspected of terrorist activities involving explosives. The Maguire family were arrested on the basis of the results of the thin-layer chromatography analysis of ether extracts of cotton-wool swabs taken from their hands and nail scrapings. The suspects were convicted. The case was re-opened years later. It became known that the TLC tests had been carried out by an 18-year-old scientific officer who had only a few weeks' experience of using TLC, but who was said to have been working under supervision. The Court of Appeal was concerned that accidental contamination of the samples from the suspects could have occurred from other materials, for example from some pharmaceutical product, and also that the inexperienced analyst might have confused samples with standards. The evidence from the TLC tests was discredited and the convictions were quashed. Because of similar uncertainties in the forensic evidence in the 'Birmingham Six' case, this was also referred to the Court of Appeal, and again the convictions were quashed.

Although more sensitive chromatographic methods have been developed, TLC is still widely used for the identification of cannabis. The stationary phase used is a thin layer of silica that has been sprayed with silver nitrate solution and then dried. Methylbenzene (toluene) is used as the mobile phase.

TLC has retained its usefulness primarily because of its simplicity, low cost and reliability when used with control samples and selected locating agents.

Gas/liquid chromatography

Gas/liquid chromatography (GLC) is used to separate and identify very small samples of gases, liquids and volatile solids. In this technique, a vaporised sample is carried by an inert gas (the mobile phase) over the surface of a liquid (the stationary phase). A diagram of the apparatus and how it works is shown in *figure 1.9*. The mobile phase, which is called the carrier gas, flows through the column of stationary phase at a constant rate. The relatively unreactive gas nitrogen is frequently used as the carrier gas. The stationary phase is a non-volatile liquid on a solid support, for example, a long-chain alkane of high boiling point coated onto the surface of SiO_2. GLC is partition chromatography – see pages 2 and 3 and *figure 1.4a*.

The components of the mixture are partitioned between the mobile and stationary phases to different extents, so that they move through the column at different rates depending on (i) their volatility and (ii) their relative solubilities in the mobile and stationary phases. When the stationary phase is non-polar the rate of movement of each component through the column is determined principally by its volatility, which is related to boiling point. But when the stationary phase is polar it will tend to retain polar components. For example, if a mixture of non-polar octane (C_8H_{18}) and polar pentanol ($C_5H_{11}OH$) is separated using a polar stationary phase, the octane would leave the column before the pentanol. Stationary phases, that is, the non-volatile liquids coated onto the solid support, are selected for their suitability for the separation of different substances.

The components of a mixture leave the column after definite intervals of time, characteristic of each component, and are monitored by a detector designed to record changes in the composition of the carrier gas as the components are separated.

Figure 1.10 shows a diagram of a chromatogram for a mixture of liquids. The time taken for each of these components to pass through the column is found by measuring the distance on the chromatogram between

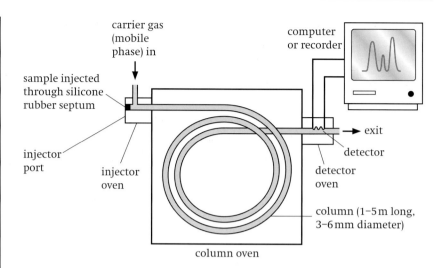

● **Figure 1.9** A gas/liquid chromatograph. The oven is needed to keep the temperature constant.

the injection of the mixture (defined as 0 minutes) and the centre of the peak for that component. We call this value the **retention time**. Since each solute has its own retention time, we can identify an unknown compound by comparing its retention time with the retention times of known compounds. However, remember that the conditions used in the experiments with unknown compounds and with known reference samples must be the same:

■ the same carrier gas;
■ the same flow rate;
■ the same stationary phase;
■ the same temperature.

The gas/liquid chromatogram also tells us how much of each component is present in the mixture. The *area* under a component peak in the chromatogram is related to the *amount* of that component in the mixture.

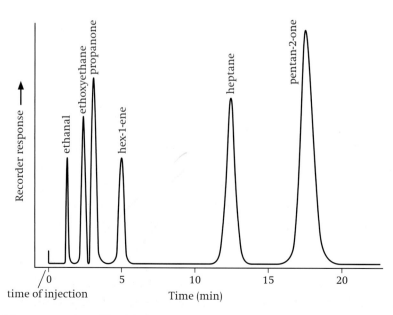

● **Figure 1.10** A gas/liquid chromatogram of a mix of organic compounds.

Another way of identifying the separated solutes as they emerge from the column is by linking the GLC apparatus to a mass spectrometer. In chapter 2 of this book you will see that the mass spectrum of a substance is like a fingerprint – the heights and distribution of the peaks in the mass spectrum will identify a substance. This technique is very sensitive, and any two solutes that can be separated with a time gap of *one second* on a GLC column can be identified almost instantly by the mass spectrometer without first being collected. Identification is by comparison with the mass spectra of known compounds, using a computer library search. This arrangement is used for analysing complex mixtures, for example for identifying the hydrocarbons in a sample of crude oil.

Determination of the percentage composition of a mixture by GLC

For quantitative analysis the component peaks are first identified and then the area of each is measured (area of peak = $\frac{1}{2}$ base × height). However, the GLC machine usually measures the area of the peak automatically and prints the results with the chromatogram. If the peaks are very narrow then peak height may be used instead of peak area. Look at *figure 1.11*, which shows the chromatogram and printout giving the peak areas for an impure compound that was tested for purity by GLC. For this method:

- the chromatogram must show peaks for all the components in the mixture;
- all the components of the mixture must be separated;
- the detector must respond equally to the different components so that peak area is directly proportional to the component concentration.

The amount of each component in the mixture is found by expressing it as a percentage of the sum of the areas of all the peaks. For example, for a mixture of three ketones A, B and C:

$$\% \text{ of ketone A} = \frac{\text{peak area of A}}{\text{sum of the areas of A, B and C}} \times 100$$

The percentage of ketones B and C can be found in the same way.

A modification of the GLC process uses an open tubular column of greater length (10–50 m) and smaller internal diameter (0.25–0.32 mm) (*figure 1.12*) than the packed column (length 1–5 m, diameter 3–6 mm) (see *figure 1.9*). The open tubular column is called a **capillary column**. This method has the advantage of increasing the sensitivity, resolution and speed of the analysis. *Figure 1.13* shows the chromatograms obtained for the separation of perfume oil using the two different types of column with the same stationary phase.

GLC is used for testing for steroids in competing athletes and for testing the fuels used in Formula One motor racing (*figure 1.14*). It is also used for medical purposes where it has been found possible to determine the percentages of dissolved oxygen, nitrogen, carbon

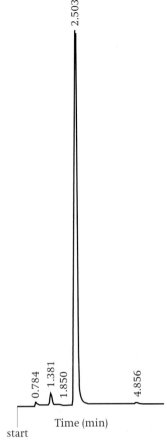

RT	Area %
0.784	0.27846
1.381	2.35848
1.850	0.09042
2.503	96.37168
4.856	0.90098

● **Figure 1.11** The chromatogram and printout for a compound tested for purity by GLC.

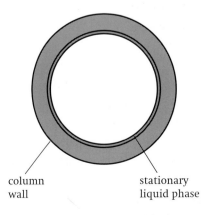

● **Figure 1.12** An open tubular column for GLC.

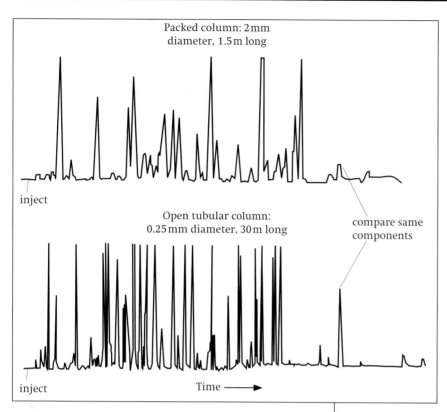

Packed column: 2 mm
diameter, 1.5 m long

inject

Open tubular column:
0.25 mm diameter, 30 m long

compare same
components

inject

Time

● **Figure 1.13** Chromatograms showing the separation of perfume oil using the two different types of column.

● **Figure 1.14** A Formula One car being refuelled. GLC is used to test the fuel, checking that the amounts of additives and performance-enhancing compounds are within allowed limits.

dioxide and carbon monoxide in blood samples as small as $1\,cm^3$. An interesting example of the use of the combined technique of GLC and mass spectrometry in forensic science is the case of a husband who killed his wife while she was a patient in hospital. He poisoned her with cyanide and then had her body cremated. However, the police found strands

of the victim's hair on a hospital pillow and detected cyanide in the hair follicles. This led to a criminal conviction.

SAQ 1.3

For GLC separations explain:

a how retention time is measured;

b how the areas under the component peaks are used.

SAQ 1.4

Select a suitable chromatographic technique for the separation of each of the following mixtures:

a a solution of sugars;

b North Sea oil;

c a solution of carbohydrates of high molecular mass.

Box 1A High-performance liquid chromatography

When we want to separate small samples of *non*-volatile substances and find out how much of each component is present, we use high-performance liquid chromatography (HPLC). This is an improved form of the original chromatography method used to separate plant pigments. It is similar to GLC except that the mobile phase is a liquid that moves under high pressure through a column containing the stationary phase. The chromatogram produced resembles a GLC chromatogram in the information it gives us. The technique is used by UK Sport to detect the presence of the stimulant caffeine in competing athletes (*figure 1.15*).

● **Figure 1.15** HPLC is used to test the urine of athletes for banned compounds such as steroids and stimulants such as caffeine.

SAQ 1.5

A gas/liquid chromatogram of the alcohols found in the space above the beer in a beer can showed the presence of ethanol, butan-1-ol, methanol and 2-methylbutan-1-ol (*figure 1.16*).

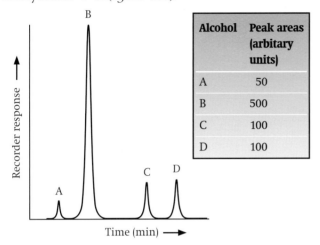

Alcohol	Peak areas (arbitary units)
A	50
B	500
C	100
D	100

● **Figure 1.16** A gas/liquid chromatogram of the vapour found above the beer in a beer can.

a Suggest which peak on the chromatogram was formed by each alcohol.

b Determine the percentage composition of each alcohol in the mixture of alcohols.

Electrophoresis

Electrophoresis involves the movement of ions in an electric field. In **zone electrophoresis**, which is described here (*figure 1.17*), the mixture is in solution but is supported on a solid or a gel. The supporting medium may consist of a strip of *filter paper* (cellulose) or a strip of *cellulose acetate*. A thin layer of *agar* or *polyacrylamide gel* may also be used. *Figure 1.18* shows the separated components of a protein mixture on the supporting medium, and this is called an **electropherogram**. Zone electrophoresis is a simple process, which effectively separates different components according to their charge and size.

■ The more highly charged an ion, the faster it moves in an electric field.

■ The larger the ion, the more slowly it moves across the supporting medium.

During electrophoresis, the temperature must be controlled, as the rate of movement of the components increases with increasing temperature. In the same way as in paper chromatography, colourless components are detected by treating the surface of the gel with chemicals or by using ultraviolet radiation. Amino acids and proteins have been extensively studied by this technique, which will work with small samples.

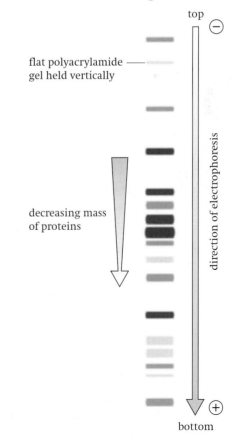

● **Figure 1.18** An electropherogram of proteins on polyacrylamide gel. The separated proteins are made visible by staining with Coomassie Blue.

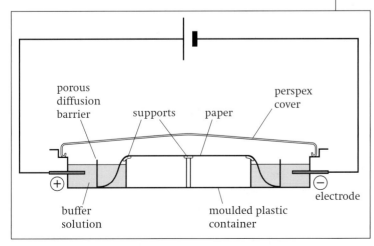

● **Figure 1.17** An apparatus for paper electrophoresis. Note the use of a buffer solution. (See *Chemistry 2*, chapter 14, for more information about pH and buffers.)

Effect of pH on electrophoresis

Figure 1.17 shows that a **buffer solution** is used as the electrolyte in order to keep the pH of the medium at a constant value during electrophoresis. This is because the net charge on the ions being separated may depend on the pH. Buffers are solutions that have been made to have a particular pH and they are capable of maintaining that pH value when small amounts of acids and bases are added to them (see *Chemistry 2*, chapter 14).

An amino acid contains at least one amino group ($-NH_2$), which is a base, and at least one carboxyl group ($-COOH$), which is an acid, for example aminoethanoic acid (glycine).

$$H_2N - \overset{\overset{\displaystyle H}{|}}{\underset{\underset{\displaystyle H}{|}}{C}} - C \overset{\displaystyle O}{\underset{\displaystyle OH}{<}}$$

In aqueous solution this acid exists largely in the form:

$$\overset{+}{H_3N} - \overset{\overset{\displaystyle H}{|}}{\underset{\underset{\displaystyle H}{|}}{C}} - C \overset{\displaystyle O}{\underset{\displaystyle O^-}{<}}$$

This is called a **zwitterion** (meaning hybrid ion, see *Chemistry 2*, chapter 5). If acid is added to this solution, the $-COO^-$ groups become protonated:

$$\overset{+}{H_3N} - \overset{\overset{\displaystyle H}{|}}{\underset{\underset{\displaystyle H}{|}}{C}} - C \overset{\displaystyle O}{\underset{\displaystyle O^-}{<}} + H^+ \rightarrow \overset{+}{H_3N} - \overset{\overset{\displaystyle H}{|}}{\underset{\underset{\displaystyle H}{|}}{C}} - C \overset{\displaystyle O}{\underset{\displaystyle OH}{<}}$$

and the zwitterion acts as a base (proton acceptor). The molecules would then have a net positive charge and would move towards the negative electrode (cathode) in an electrophoresis experiment.

If a base is added to the solution, the $-\overset{+}{N}H_3$ groups lose a proton:

$$\overset{+}{H_3N} - \overset{\overset{\displaystyle H}{|}}{\underset{\underset{\displaystyle H}{|}}{C}} - C \overset{\displaystyle O}{\underset{\displaystyle O^-}{<}} + OH^- \rightarrow H_2N - \overset{\overset{\displaystyle H}{|}}{\underset{\underset{\displaystyle H}{|}}{C}} - C \overset{\displaystyle O}{\underset{\displaystyle O^-}{<}} + H_2O$$

and the zwitterion acts as an acid (proton donor). The molecules now have a net negative charge and would move to the positive electrode (anode).

If changes in pH were to occur during the separation process, the direction of movement of the amino acids could be reversed, which is why the buffer solution is so important.

SAQ 1.6

What factors determine the rate of movement of molecules during electrophoresis?

SAQ 1.7

a Write down the formula for the form in which pure valine

$$\begin{array}{c} CH_3 \\ | \\ H_3C - \overset{|}{C} - H \\ | \\ H_2N - \overset{|}{\underset{\underset{\displaystyle H}{|}}{C}} - C \overset{\displaystyle O}{\underset{\displaystyle OH}{<}} \end{array}$$

would mainly exist in aqueous solution.

b How would this change if a small amount of hydrogen ions were added?

Electrophoresis in the analysis of genes

Genetic studies have shown that living cells carry sets of information or codes for building up proteins. These codes, which determine the sequence of amino acids in proteins, are stored in large molecules called nucleic acids. There are two general types of nucleic acid – DNA (deoxyribonucleic acid) and RNA (ribonucleic acid).

■ The DNA double helix consists of two twisted strands made up of alternating sugar (deoxyribose) and phosphate groups. A base is attached to each sugar group. The bases in DNA are adenine (A), thymine (T), guanine (G) and cytosine (C).

■ RNA is a single-stranded chain, containing A, G, C and uracil (U). In RNA the sugar is ribose.

A chromosome is a very long chain of DNA containing a sequence of discrete sections called genes *(figure 1.19)*. Genes are the units of heredity. Each gene carries a code, which may direct the synthesis of a specific protein molecule; genes are responsible for characteristics such as hair colour and height and for diseases such as cystic fibrosis.

The double helix of DNA is held together by hydrogen bonds between the bases in the two strands. Thymine bonds to adenine by two hydrogen bonds and cytosine bonds to guanine by three hydrogen bonds: this is called base pairing *(figure 1.20)*. The general chemical structure of the DNA of every person is the same; the only difference between the DNA of different people is the order (or sequence) of the base pairs.

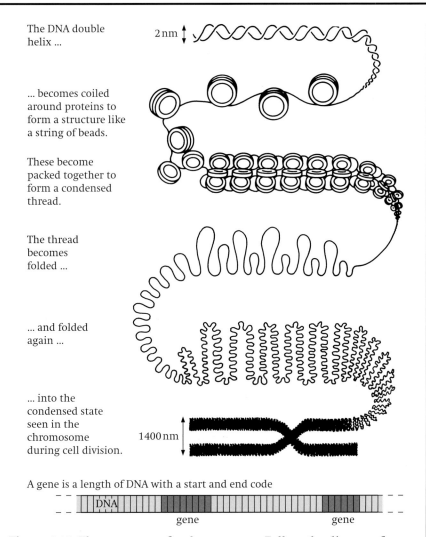

The DNA double helix ...

2 nm

... becomes coiled around proteins to form a structure like a string of beads.

These become packed together to form a condensed thread.

The thread becomes folded ...

... and folded again ...

... into the condensed state seen in the chromosome during cell division.

1400 nm

A gene is a length of DNA with a start and end code

DNA

gene   gene

● **Figure 1.19** The structure of a chromosome. Follow the diagram from the top (the DNA double helix) to the bottom (the chromosome).

The history of genetic fingerprinting (DNA profiling)

Genetic fingerprinting as a test was developed at the University of Leicester by Professor Alec Jeffreys in 1984. He found that there are segments in genes and segments between genes that do not carry instructions for the manufacture of proteins. These 'useless' pieces of DNA consist of short sequences of about 10–15 base-pairs (see *figure 1.20*) and they are repeated in different parts of the DNA strand. They are called minisatellites. Minisatellites exist in everyone's DNA, but the number and pattern of repeats are different for each person. Only in the case of identical twins would these

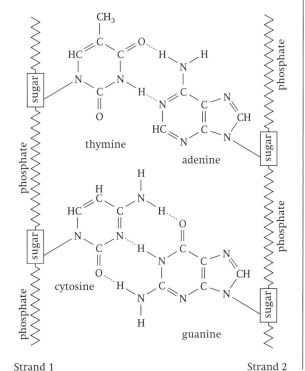

● **Figure 1.20** Base pairing in the structure of DNA. The hydrogen bonds, represented here by ..., are formed between two bases, one from each strand.

thymine

adenine

cytosine

guanine

Strand 1

Strand 2

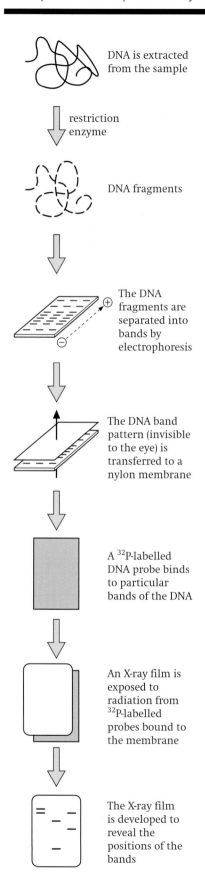

DNA is extracted from the sample

restriction enzyme

DNA fragments

The DNA fragments are separated into bands by electrophoresis

The DNA band pattern (invisible to the eye) is transferred to a nylon membrane

A ³²P-labelled DNA probe binds to particular bands of the DNA

An X-ray film is exposed to radiation from ³²P-labelled probes bound to the membrane

The X-ray film is developed to reveal the positions of the bands

● **Figure 1.21** The steps in the process of genetic fingerprinting.

be the same. We inherit half of these minisatellite regions from our mother and half from our father. The genetic fingerprint is made from the minisatellite regions.

Making a genetic fingerprint (DNA profiling)

The steps followed in genetic fingerprinting are outlined in *figure 1.21*. About 20 mg of DNA are required to make a genetic fingerprint. The sample may be taken from any source that contains cells, for example bone, blood, hair roots, saliva or semen. The DNA is extracted from the chromosomes in the cells' nuclei. The long DNA molecules are then split into smaller fragments by treating them with **restriction enzymes**. These restriction enzymes recognise specific sequences in the DNA and cut the strands like ' chemical scissors' at specific places.

The DNA fragments in the mixture are then separated by electrophoresis on a gel. DNA fragments from different sources are placed in separate lanes in the gel and subjected to an electric current. The fragments are negatively charged and move towards the positive electrode. The size of a fragment determines how fast it moves, with smaller fragments moving faster and further in the electric field than the larger ones.

The separated fragments on the gel are then transferred to a nylon membrane to preserve their relative positions and are heat-treated to form single-stranded DNA. Specially prepared sequences of DNA labelled with radioactive phosphorus-32 are applied to the nylon membrane, and these stick to the minisatellite sequences on the DNA fragments. To make the positions of the fragments visible, an X-ray film is placed next to the nylon membrane. The radioactive tags attached to the fragments cause fogging of the film, and this creates a pattern of bands. This is the genetic fingerprint, and it resembles a bar code found on retail goods. The length of each DNA fragment is found by running DNA fragments of known length alongside the test sample and comparing the distances they migrate across the gel.

For many investigations, this method of genetic fingerprinting is no longer considered to be adequate. Relatively large samples of DNA are required, which may not always be available. Also, the sample of DNA to be tested can become contaminated, for example with the blue dye from denim jeans. In this case, the dye can combine with the restriction enzymes, causing them to cut the DNA in the wrong places and so create too few or too many fragments.

A new method of DNA profiling is now preferred, known as **short tandem repeat analysis** (see *box 1C*).

Some applications of genetic fingerprinting
Establishing relationships

Figure 1.24 (page 14) shows how parenthood can be established by genetic fingerprinting. However, errors may arise and cast doubt on the reliability of the method. For example, DNA decays rapidly.

Box 1C Short tandem repeat analysis

Short tandem repeats (STRs) is the name given to locations on the chromosome that contain short sequences which repeat themselves in the DNA molecule (see *figure 1.22*). The DNA is extracted from the biological sample and a selected STR is copied by a powerful technique called the **polymerase chain reaction** (see *box 1D*, page 15). Over a million copies of the selected STR can be produced. The STRs are then separated by electrophoresis. A probe designed to bind to the DNA sequence at one point only is used to locate the bands. A radioactive probe or one that provides a fluorescent stain in ultraviolet light may be used. The resulting genetic pattern consists of two bands. This is because every person has two types of a particular STR, which differ in their number of repeats. One is inherited from each parent. By measuring the distance the STRs have moved in the electrophoretic gel and comparing them with control samples and size markers we can find the number of repeats in the STRs. Usually a number of different STRs in the sample are simultaneously extracted, copied and detected. *Figure 1.23* shows the profile of six bands from three different STRs. The frequency of the occurrence of this profile in the population is then measured and the probability of finding two matching profiles by chance is calculated.

STR analysis is more discriminating than the fingerprinting method opposite. Also, the short strands of DNA used are more stable and less likely to be degraded than longer strands. They can be removed from stains and bodies where decomposition has already occurred. The process is also much quicker and tiny samples of DNA can be copied so that a genetic profile may be obtained from as little as 1 ng (1×10^{-9} g) of DNA, a single cell or a flake of dandruff.

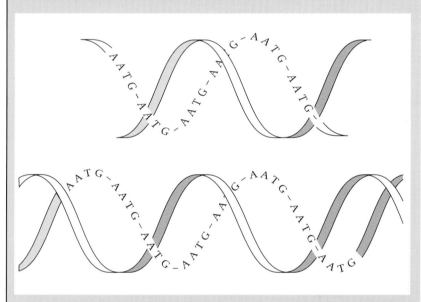

● **Figure 1.22** A diagram showing two variants of a short tandem repeat (STR). The DNA segments contain the repeating sequence -A-A-T-G-. One strand of DNA contains six repeats of the -A-A-T-G- sequence, while the other contains eight repeats. The number of repeats is determined by the distance the STR moves on the gel during electrophoresis.

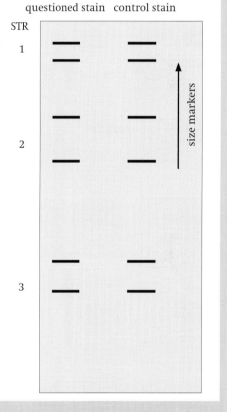

● **Figure 1.23** A DNA profile.

When this happens, some of the DNA sites that would normally be cut by the restriction enzyme may no longer be available. So, too few or too many fragments may be formed.

In small communities or small ethnic groups, where people marry among themselves, they become closely related genetically. A child may then inherit an identical DNA sequence (minisatellite) from each parent. The result is that the child's genetic fingerprint will show one dark band in place of two lighter ones. Only identical twins would give exactly the same fingerprint.

A use in medicine

Doctors now use genetic fingerprinting in the treatment of leukaemia, which is a cancer of the bone marrow. Bone marrow makes new blood cells; if it becomes diseased, it can be removed and replaced

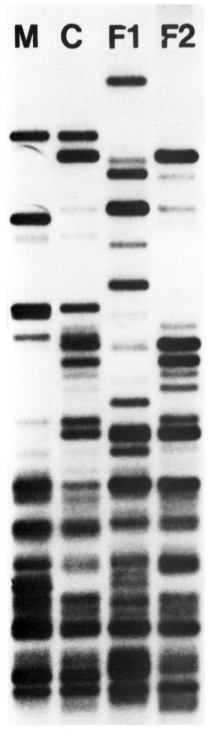

by transplanted bone marrow from a donor. After the operation, a genetic fingerprint of the patient's blood will show the donor's bands if the operation has been successful.

A use in archaeology

Scientists are still trying to piece together the two-thousand-years-old Dead Sea Scrolls, which have become fragmented (*figure 1.25*). This undertaking is like trying to solve a large number of jigsaw puzzles with all the jigsaws mixed up in the same box. However, each scroll is believed to have been made from the skin of one animal, a sheep or a goat, so genetic fingerprinting can identify the fragments belonging to a particular scroll and speed up the reconstruction of the precious documents.

Forensic testing

Genetic profiling is a very useful technique for the detection of crime. Samples from suspects are taken by the police, who swab the inside of the suspect's cheek. The Forensic Science Service then analyses the DNA in the sample and the suspect's genetic profile is produced. This is compared with a profile obtained from a biological sample found at the scene of the crime. Genetic profiling is

● **Figure 1.24** Labelled genetic 'fingerprints' showing how parenthood is established. By matching the child's bands (C) with those of the mother (M) and the possible father, F2 is seen to be the child's real father.

● **Figure 1.25** A reconstruction of part of the Dead Sea Scrolls.

based on the principle of exclusion. A single difference between the pattern of a suspect and the scene of crime sample can exonerate that suspect.

There is always the possibility that the samples may match by chance. However, it has been found that the frequency of occurrence of some profiles is so low that the probability of getting a match is only 1 in 25 million. Britain also has a DNA database. Here the DNA profiles of all persons who have been convicted of a criminal offence are stored, as well as the DNA profiles of samples taken from crime scenes. Access to these profiles enables the police to identify suspects with previous convictions for rape, burglary and murder, for example, and also to eliminate innocent people from their enquiries.

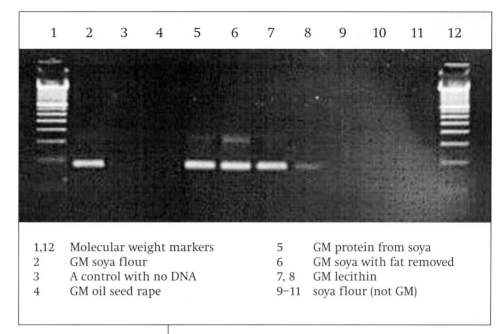

1,12	Molecular weight markers	5	GM protein from soya
2	GM soya flour	6	GM soya with fat removed
3	A control with no DNA	7, 8	GM lecithin
4	GM oil seed rape	9–11	soya flour (not GM)

● **Figure 1.26** GM soya can be detected by DNA analysis.

SAQ 1.8

How and why is electrophoresis used in DNA fingerprinting/profiling?

Detecting genetically modified (GM) foods

GM foods originate from plants that have been given particular characteristics by introducing special genes into them. For example a 'foreign' gene can be inserted into the soya plant to make the plant resistant to a specific herbicide. This herbicide can then be used on the crop and it is only the soya plants that survive. The weeds are killed and a higher yield of crop is obtained. About 65% of foods contain soya and in 1998 the European Commission ruled that all food containing GM soya must be labelled. Genetic modifications may be detected by DNA analysis. The DNA is extracted from the food sample and the polymerase chain reaction is used to form millions of copies of the GM DNA fragments. These are then identified by gel electrophoresis (*figure 1.26* and *box 1D*).

Precautions

Great care must be taken in avoiding contamination in DNA fingerprinting/profiling. Certain contaminants can combine with restriction enzymes and so create too few or too many fragments. Other contaminants may affect the charge on the fragments and consequently the position of the bands on the fingerprint. In STR profiling (see *box 1C*) where very small samples of DNA are used (one or two cells) stringent precautions in collecting and processing the DNA are employed to avoid contamination with DNA from other sources.

Box 1D The polymerase chain reaction

The polymerase chain reaction (PCR) is used to copy specific DNA sequences using the enzyme DNA polymerase. In this process the DNA is mixed with short specially designed pieces of DNA called primers, the enzyme DNA polymerase and the four bases (A, T, G, C) that are the building blocks of DNA. This mixture is subjected to a cycle of thermal changes during which:

1 the double-stranded DNA is separated into single strands;

2 the primers become attached to either side of the target sequence and direct the enzyme to copy only the target DNA;

3 the enzyme directs the rebuilding of the double strand by adding on the bases so that two complete pairs of double-stranded DNA are formed.

This cycle is repeated until sufficient copies of the target DNA have been made.

SUMMARY

◆ Chromatography and electrophoresis separate substances for identification.

◆ In chromatography, the mobile phase moves the components of a mixture through or over the stationary phase. Separation occurs by the transfer of the components to the stationary phase either by partition between two liquids, by partition between a gas and a liquid or by adsorption on to a solid surface.

◆ The stationary phase may be solid or liquid; the mobile phase may be liquid or gas.

◆ In paper and thin-layer chromatography the components of a mixture are identified by their R_f values.

◆ Two-way chromatography can be used to aid the separation of components. The initial chromatogram is rotated by 90° and a second separation is carried out using a different solvent.

◆ In gas/liquid chromatography the components of a mixture are identified by their retention times; the amount of each is found by measuring the area of each peak.

◆ Chromatography is used for the analysis of a wide variety of substances, for example hydrocarbon oils, vitamins, steroids, amino acids, peptides and sugars. It is used in the petroleum and food industries and in forensic and medical testing.

◆ In zone electrophoresis, the mixture to be separated is supported on a solid gel or framework. The components of the mixture are charged and move in an applied electric field, where they separate according to their charge and their size.

◆ A buffer solution is used as the electrolyte in electrophoresis. For any species, particularly for amino acids and proteins, the net charge on the molecule depends on the pH of the electrolyte.

◆ Electrophoresis is used in the production of genetic fingerprints/profiles.

◆ Genetic fingerprints/profiles are used in establishing parenthood.

◆ In forensic science, DNA profiles are made from samples of body fluids or tissue taken from the 'scene of crime' and these are compared with samples from suspects.

◆ DNA fingerprinting/profiling has applications in many other branches of science, among them medicine, archaeology and the detection of GM foods.

Questions

1 For the separation of mixtures of organic solutes in solution, explain the following.
   a How does solute separation occur in
      (i) paper chromatography
      (ii) thin-layer chromatography?
   b How can the solutes be positively identified on the chromatogram?

2 For GLC separations:
   a explain what is meant by the terms mobile phase and stationary phase
   b explain how the components of the mixture are separated on the chromatography column.

3 Buffer solutions are usually used as the electrolyte in electrophoresis. Explain why this is done.

4 a List the sequence of the steps in the genetic or DNA fingerprinting process.
   b Name two applications of genetic or DNA fingerprinting/profiling and comment on the reliability of the results.

CHAPTER 2

Mass spectrometry

By the end of this chapter you should be able to:

1 recall the basic features of a mass spectrometer and understand how a mass spectrum is produced;

2 use accurate relative molecular mass data from high-resolution mass spectrometry to distinguish between molecules of similar relative molecular mass;

3 suggest the identity of the major fragment ions in a given mass spectrum;

4 use molecular ion peaks, base peaks and fragmentation peaks to identify structures;

5 use the M and $[M + 1]$ peaks from a mass spectrum to determine the number of carbon atoms in a molecule of an organic molecule;

6 use the M, $[M + 2]$ and $[M + 4]$ peaks from a mass spectrum to identify organic compounds containing chlorine and bromine.

In 1919 Francis Aston produced his first mass spectrometer – an instrument for determining the mass of an atom (*figure 2.1*). He examined positive ions from neon and found that there were two types of ion present, with relative isotopic masses of 20 and 22. He had found a way of separating and identifying isotopes. Since then,

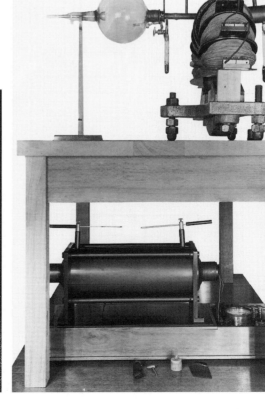

● **Figure 2.1**
a F. W. Aston (1877–1945).
b The first mass spectrometer, built by Aston at Cambridge, UK.

the method has been developed so that it is now a very valuable tool for analysing atoms and molecules of gases, liquids and solids.

In your earlier studies, you will have seen how mass spectrometry can be used to find the masses of isotopes and their relative abundances (see *Chemistry 1*, chapter 2) and to determine relative molecular masses (see *Chemistry 2*, chapter 8). In this chapter we will find out more about how the mass spectrometer works and examine some of its applications in more detail.

The mass spectrometer

Any substance that can be vaporised without decomposing may be analysed by mass spectrometry. *Figure 2.2* shows how a mass spectrometer works. Notice the vacuum pump, which removes atmospheric gases from the apparatus before the sample is injected. This vacuum is necessary because the molecules of these unwanted gases could collide with the ions and break them up further. Also the atmospheric gases would be detected by the spectrometer and appear in the spectrum. A mass spectrometer works at a pressure of 1×10^{-7} kPa, as compared to normal atmospheric pressure of 100 kPa.

Processes that occur in the ionisation chamber

Atoms

The electron beam bombards the atoms and removes one electron (or occasionally two) from the outermost shells to form positive ions. We will only consider the case when one electron is removed. For example, for neon:

$$Ne + e^- \rightarrow Ne^+ + 2e^-$$

Molecules

The molecules are first ionised by bombardment with the beam of high-energy electrons. For example, for butanone:

$$CH_3COCH_2CH_3 + e^- \rightarrow [CH_3COCH_2CH_3]^+ + 2e^-$$

The ion produced is called the molecular ion, M^+. During the bombardment, some energy is transferred to the molecular ions produced by the collisions. This weakens the bonds in the ions and some of them break apart. We say that the ions **fragment** into smaller pieces, one of which carries the charge and the other of which is neutral (carries no net charge). Again, for butanone:

$$[CH_3COCH_2CH_3]^+ \rightarrow [CH_3COCH_2]^+ + CH_3\bullet$$

These fragments may in turn break into smaller pieces. It is the fragments that carry a positive charge which are detected by the spectrometer.

Analysis of the ions

Look at *figure 2.2* and follow the progress of the singly charged positive ions through the instrument.

■ The ions are accelerated by the electric field and concentrated into a narrow beam by the electric field.

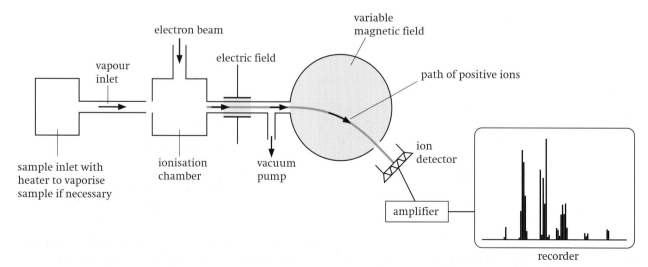

● **Figure 2.2** A schematic diagram of a modern mass spectrometer.

- The ions enter the magnetic field, which causes them to move in circular paths. The strength of the magnetic field is varied so that ions of differing mass-to-charge (m/e) ratios are deflected into the detector. The lightest ions are the most readily deflected and require the smallest magnetic field to 'focus' them on the detector.
- The strength of the magnetic field is gradually increased, so that ions of increasing mass are focused successively onto the ion detector.
- An electric current is produced when ions strike the detector. For ions of a given m/e value, the detector current is proportional to the relative abundance of that type of ion in the sample being analysed.
- The detector currents are recorded as a series of peaks. This is the mass spectrum.

For the mass spectra of elements, it is the **natural abundance** of the isotopes (also called the absolute abundance) that is plotted against their mass-to-charge (m/e) ratio. *Figure 2.3* shows the mass spectrum of krypton.

The mass spectra of compounds are usually recorded as line diagrams of **relative abundance** plotted against m/e ratio, on which only the major peaks are shown. The abundance of each fragment ion is represented as a percentage of the most abundant (stable) fragment, which is called the **base peak**. The base peak, by convention, has a relative abundance of 100%. Some examples are shown later in this chapter.

The mass spectra of compounds are as unique as fingerprints; it is very unlikely that two different compounds will fragment in exactly the same way. Mass spectra are used in oil refineries for comparison in the analysis of complex hydrocarbon mixtures (*figure 2.4*). But remember that for the comparisons to be accurate, the conditions used in the experiments must be the same, that is:

- the same temperature;
- the same ionising voltage;
- the same type of instrument (or one calibrated for comparison).

Mass spectrometers have also been placed in rockets to study the chemistry of outer space!

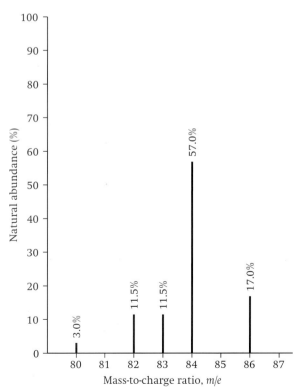

- **Figure 2.3** A mass spectrum of krypton, showing the natural abundance of the various isotopes.

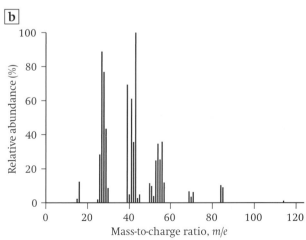

- **Figure 2.4** The analysis of a complex hydrocarbon mixture from an oil refinery (**a**) may give a mass spectrum like that shown (**b**).

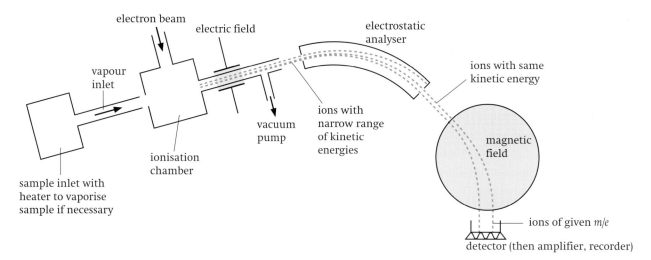

- **Figure 2.5** A schematic diagram of a high-resolution (double-focussing) mass spectrometer.

High-resolution (double-focussing) mass spectrometer

Many modern mass spectrometers contain an additional device known as an **electrostatic analyser** (*figure 2.5*). Ions that have been accelerated by an electric field do not have identical kinetic energies and this energy spread limits the resolution of the magnetic analyser. The electrostatic analyser consists of two curved electrostatically charged plates which focus the ions into one very narrow kinetic energy range before they enter the variable magnetic field. This 'double focussing' greatly increases the resolution of the instrument, so that atomic masses can be determined to an accuracy of one part in 10^6. This enables the molecular formulae of compounds to be found, as discussed below.

Applications of mass spectrometry

Determination of relative atomic mass

We know that most chemical elements are mixtures of **isotopes** and that the abundances of the individual isotopes of a particular element are nearly always in a constant ratio. The **relative atomic mass** of such mixtures, that is the A_r of any element, is defined as the ratio of the weighted average of the various relative isotopic masses present to $\frac{1}{12}$ of the mass of the carbon-12 isotope (^{12}C). Relative atomic mass is discussed more fully in *Chemistry 1*, chapter 2.

Figure 2.3 shows you that the relative isotopic masses and the isotopic abundances may be read directly from the mass spectrum. We can use such data to calculate the relative atomic mass of this sample of krypton:

$$A_r = \frac{80 \times 3.0 + 82 \times 11.5 + 83 \times 11.5 + 84 \times 57.0 + 86 \times 17.0}{100}$$

$$= 83.9$$

Determination of relative molecular mass and molecular formulae

The **molecular ion** M^+ formed by the loss of one electron from a whole molecule (i.e. no fragmentation) produces the peak with the highest m/e value in a mass spectrum. Using a high-resolution mass spectrometer (see above), we can find very accurate masses for the M^+ ions and hence work out their molecular formulae.

For example, the simple ions N_2^+ and CO^+ are both recorded on low-resolution mass spectra at an m/e value of 28 (written in short as m/e 28). However, with a high-resolution mass spectrometer, accurate relative molecular masses of 28.0061 and 27.9949, respectively, are found. This means that the two ions can be distinguished; and they can be identified by using the accurate values for isotopic atomic masses shown in *table 2.1*.

Tables of molecular masses accurate to several decimal places have been compiled for comparison with unknown molecules, so that the mass spectrometer provides a quick method of determining a molecular formula. It has the added advantage

Isotope	Relative isotopic mass
hydrogen	1.0078
carbon-12	12.0000
nitrogen-14	14.0031
oxygen-16	15.9949

● **Table 2.1**

that only a small amount of the substance is needed for the analysis.

SAQ 2.1

The high-resolution mass spectrum of a volatile mixture showed peaks at m/e 42.0468 and 44.0261. Identify the components of this mixture, using the accurate relative isotopic masses in *table 2.1*.

Finding the number of carbon atoms in an organic molecule using M and $[M + 1]$ peaks

Look at the mass spectrum of ethanol in *figure 2.6*. Notice the small peak at m/e 47 next to the molecular-ion peak M at m/e 46. This peak at m/e 47 corresponds to what we call the $[M + 1]^+$ **molecular ion**. An $[M + 1]$ peak appears in the mass spectra of all organic compounds because some of the molecules contain the naturally occurring carbon-13 isotope (^{13}C). Carbon-13 is present with a natural abundance of 1.10% of carbon-12. Carbon-13 is a non-radioactive isotope of carbon – unlike the ^{14}C isotope, which is radioactive (see later).

The number of carbon atoms in the molecule is reflected in the height of the $[M + 1]$ peak. For example, if the molecule contains three carbon atoms, the height of the $[M + 1]$ peak would be approximately 3.30% of the height of the molecular-ion peak, because there is a 1.10% probability that any one of three carbon atoms is the carbon-13 isotope. A calculation involving M and $[M + 1]$ peaks is shown on page 23.

Interpretation of the mass spectrum of ethanol

We have seen that molecules fragment in the mass spectrometer owing to the impact of high-energy electrons. By identifying these fragments, we can suggest possible structures for the original molecules.

The mass spectrum of ethanol, C_2H_5OH, is shown in *figure 2.6*. This spectrum can be interpreted as follows:

- m/e 47, $[M + 1]$; this peak has a height approximately 2.20% of the height of the M peak, confirming the presence of two carbon atoms in the ethanol molecule

- m/e 46, M

$$C_2H_5OH + e^- \rightarrow [C_2H_5OH]^+ + 2e^-$$

- m/e 45, $[C_2H_5O]^+$

$$[C_2H_5OH]^+ \rightarrow [C_2H_5O]^+ + H\cdot$$

- m/e 31, $[CH_2OH]^+$

$$[C_2H_5OH]^+ \rightarrow [CH_2OH]^+ + CH_3\cdot$$

- m/e 29, $[C_2H_5]^+$

$$[C_2H_5OH]^+ \rightarrow [C_2H_5]^+ + OH\cdot$$

- m/e 27, $[C_2H_3]^+$

$$[C_2H_5OH]^+ \rightarrow [C_2H_3]^+ + H_3O\cdot$$

We would normally expect the peak with the greatest m/e value to represent the molecular ion. However, this is not always the case – due to fragmentation, the molecular-ion peak may be absent.

The mass of a fragment will not be recorded on a mass spectrum unless the fragment carries a charge.

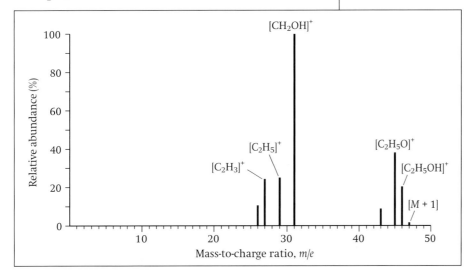

● **Figure 2.6** The mass spectrum of ethanol.

Box 2A Carbon-14 dating

Estimating the age of ancient objects is important to archaeologists and historians (*figure 2.11*). This may be done by measuring the amount of carbon-14 present in the specimen. Carbon-14 is a radioactive isotope of carbon. The carbon-14 present may be measured by mass spectrometry, which is the quicker method, or by measuring the intensity of the radiation emitted, which is proportional to the concentration of carbon-14 in the specimen.

Carbon-14 is formed continuously in the atmosphere by the action of cosmic radiation on nitrogen. In all *living* things the ratio of carbon-14 to carbon-12 is constant, but when a plant or animal dies the amount of carbon-14 starts to decrease. This is because the carbon-14 undergoes radioactive decay, and the dead plant or animal no longer takes in carbon-14 from the atmosphere. Since we know the rate at which carbon-14 decays (its half-life is 5730 years), we can estimate the length of time for which an animal or plant has been dead. (See *Chemistry 2*, chapter 12, for an explanation of half-life.)

By finding the ratio of carbon-14 to carbon-12 in samples of the Dead Sea Scrolls (which were written on animal skins) the scrolls were found to be about 2100 years old..

● **Figure 2.11** An ancient object – the Turin Shroud. This is a piece of linen cloth over 4 m long that shows an image of a crucified man. Many believe it to be the burial shroud of Christ. Linen is made from a plant called flax. The carbon atoms in the cloth come from the carbon dioxide taken up from the atmosphere while the flax plants were living. In April 1988, samples of the shroud were removed and tested. Three laboratories (in Arizona, Oxford and Zurich) each received 50 mg of the shroud, which they cleaned, burned to convert carbon in the linen to CO_2, and then reduced the CO_2 to graphite. The $^{14}C/^{13}C$ and $^{14}C/^{12}C$ ratios were then measured by mass spectrometry. The age of the samples tested was calculated to be in the range 1260–1390 AD, showing that the cloth could not have been the burial shroud of Christ.

Mass spectrometry linked to gas/liquid chromatography

We have seen in chapter 1 how the components of a complex mixture can be separated by gas/liquid chromatography. Also, we know that unknown compounds can be identified by comparing their retention time with those of known compounds. But a much more reliable method for identification is to link a mass spectrometer to a gas/liquid chromatograph and to record the mass spectrum of each component of the mixture as it emerges from the gas/liquid chromatograph. When a computer is added to this system, a further advantage is gained. The computer can record and store several hundred mass spectra and can be programmed to compare the mass spectrum of an unknown compound with the mass spectra in its memory.

Under carefully controlled conditions no two substances produce the same fragmentation pattern, so the mass spectrum produced is considered to be a 'fingerprint' of the substance being examined. This combined technique allows us to identify chemical structures quickly with the advantage that only minute amounts of the unknown substance is required.

We often need to confirm the identity of traces of toxic substances in food and water and of drugs in biological fluids. For example, mineral water bottling plants use natural spring-water. This may be contaminated with many chemicals, including herbicides and organic pesticides. Environmental protection agencies have identified over 100 compounds whose concentration must not exceed one part per billion (10^9) in bottled water. The analysis of such a low concentration of contaminants is difficult, but it can be done using mass spectrometry linked to gas/liquid chromatography.

Recently, we have seen a great deal of publicity given to the abuse of drugs in athletics. But athletics is not alone. The Horserace Forensic Testing Laboratory tests racehorses for drugs. Nowadays, most competitive sports involve drug testing. It has even been extended to bowls, and a case has been reported of an 83-year-old woman who failed a drug test because she had taken beta-blockers for her heart condition! As in the case of water analysis, mass spectrometry linked to gas/liquid chromatography is used for drug analysis.

A medical use of mass spectrometry is in the fight against cancer. For example, hormonal steroids from patients' urine samples must be analysed, but this is difficult to do because the concentration of the steroids is low and they degrade easily. However, these substances can be successfully identified with a mass spectrometer linked to gas/liquid chromatography.

There are many more applications of mass spectrometry, but the efficiency of this powerful method of analysis is perhaps best summarised by one final example: one hundred constituents of lime juice may be separated by gas/liquid chromatography and analysed by mass spectrometry within 30 minutes using only one millionth of a gram (1×10^{-6} g) of the sample.

Question

1 Explain how mass spectrometry may be used to find the following:
a accurate atomic masses
b the presence of chlorine in a compound.
c the structure of an organic compound.

SUMMARY

- In mass spectrometry, atoms and molecules in the vapour state are bombarded with a beam of high-energy electrons, forming positive ions, which may then fragment.

- The positive ions are accelerated and concentrated into a narrow beam by an electric field. They are then exposed to a magnetic field, where they are deflected. The amount each ion is deflected depends on its mass-to-charge (m/e) ratio.

- The strength of the magnetic field is gradually increased so that ions of increasing mass are focussed successively onto an ion detector.

- The detector currents are recorded as a series of peaks, producing the mass spectrum.

- The position of each peak represents the mass of the ion, and the height of a peak represents its abundance.

- A high-resolution mass spectrometer can be used to provide accurate measurement of relative molecular masses.

- Molecular formulae and molecular structures may be determined by the study of mass spectra, including analysis of the fragmentation pattern.

- The M and $[M + 1]$ molecular-ion peaks indicate the number of carbon atoms in a compound.

- The M, $[M + 2]$ and $[M + 4]$ molecular-ion peaks are useful for identifying compounds containing chlorine and bromine.

- When accurate analysis of a large number of compounds is required, a mass spectrometer is linked to a gas/liquid chromatography unit.

Atomic emission spectroscopy

In this chapter you will learn how atomic emission spectroscopy allows us to identify atoms and measure their concentrations in a sample, irrespective of how these atoms are combined (*figure 3.1*).

Before we discuss this, we will consider the electromagnetic spectrum and the nature of electromagnetic radiation.

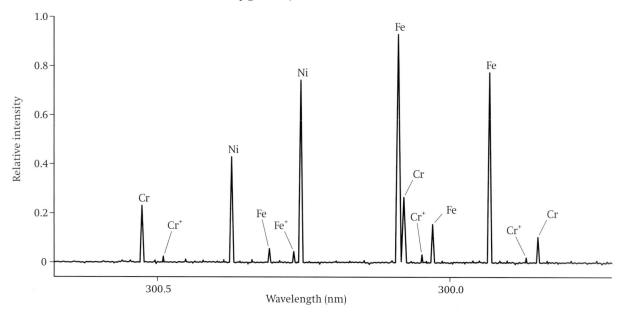

● **Figure 3.1** A very small part of the atomic spectrum of a sample of steel. The resolution is 0.001 nm.

Electromagnetic radiation

Experiments involving the interaction of electromagnetic radiation with matter has provided us with detailed knowledge of processes that occur in atoms and molecules (*figure 3.2*). Also, from your earlier studies you will know that infrared radiation (*Chemistry 1*, chapter 11, and *Chemistry 2*, chapter 8) and radiofrequencies (used in n.m.r. spectroscopy, *Chemistry 2*, chapter 8) are used to work out the structures of organic molecules.

However, electromagnetic radiation has many other uses. For example, X-rays and ultraviolet, visible and infrared radiation can be used to look below the surface of paintings, so that the materials used may be identified, the work of earlier restorers detected and deliberate forgeries exposed. *Figure 3.3* shows a fourteenth-century painting of Mary Magdalen. Examination with X-rays revealed a scroll beneath the robe of the saint that had been overpainted by another artist. At the same time, the figure had been changed to represent St. Margaret. Some time later St. Margaret was overpainted with the figure of Mary Magdalen again. Investigations such as these are important to art historians, who often want to date ancient paintings and identify the artists.

● **Figure 3.3**
a A fourteenth-century painting of Mary Magdalen, from work in Florence by the artist Allegretto Nuzzi in 1345.
b An X-ray photograph of the painting. As in human X-rays, details below the surface can be observed.

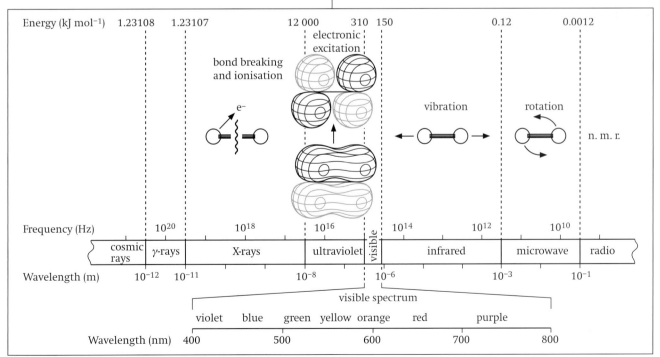

● **Figure 3.2** The electromagnetic spectrum, showing the different regions in units of wavelength, frequency and energy. These are linked to the processes that occur in atoms and molecules when different radiation is absorbed and to the various branches of spectroscopy.

Waves and particles

Electromagnetic radiation can be described in terms of both waves and particles. Look at *figure 3.4a*. This shows the 'wave' representation of electromagnetic radiation. The relation between frequency and wavelength is

$$c = f\lambda \tag{3.1}$$

where c is the speed of electromagnetic radiation in a vacuum, f = frequency and λ = wavelength. c is a constant, whatever the wavelength and frequency of the radiation, and has the value $3.00 \times 10^8 \, \text{m s}^{-1}$.

Since c is a constant and $f = c/\lambda$, then

$$f \propto \frac{1}{\lambda}$$

For example, red light has a wavelength of about 650 nm (1 nm = 1×10^{-9} m). The corresponding frequency can be calculated:

$$f = \frac{c}{\lambda}$$

$$f = \frac{3.00 \times 10^8 \, \text{m s}^{-1}}{650 \times 10^{-9} \, \text{m}}$$

$$= 4.62 \times 10^{14} \, \text{s}^{-1}$$

The unit s^{-1} is also given the special name hertz, symbol Hz.

When we want to relate electromagnetic radiation to energy, it is more convenient to consider that electromagnetic radiation consists of 'particles' or packets of energy, called **photons** (*figure 3.4b*).

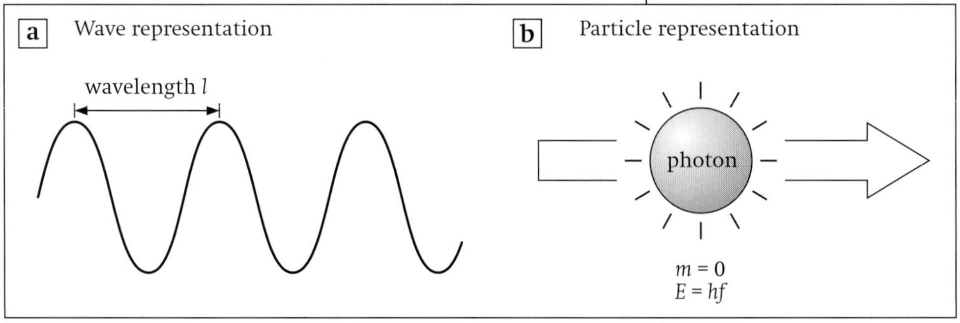

Each photon (also known as a **quantum**) carries the energy E. The relation between energy and frequency is:

$$E = hf \tag{3.2}$$

where h is the Planck constant, which has the value $6.63 \times 10^{-34} \, \text{J s}$.

Since h is a constant, then

$$E \propto f$$

When equations 3.1 and 3.2 are combined, we get:

$$E = \frac{hc}{\lambda} \tag{3.3}$$

Quantum theory

Quantum theory, which was formulated between 1900 and 1915, is due to the work of Max Planck, Niels Bohr and Albert Einstein. The basis of this theory is that a substance emits or absorbs electromagnetic radiation in multiples of small amounts (or **quanta**) of energy. The change in energy is expressed by Planck's equation:

$$E_2 - E_1 = \Delta E = hf \tag{3.4}$$

The energy is absorbed or emitted in whole-number multiples of hf, for example hf, $2hf$, $3hf$, etc. but never in fractions of hf, for example $1.4hf$ or $3.6hf$. The energy of a substance can only change from a particular value by an integral number of quanta. All types of energy exist as distinct unconnected (discrete) energy levels. Planck's equation connects the two concepts of radiation since the energy of the quantum of radiation, the photon (from the 'particle' concept) is calculated from the frequency of the radiation (from the 'wave' concept).

For example, we can calculate by how much the energy of a molecule is increased when it absorbs ultraviolet radiation of wavelength 120 nm.

(1 nm = 1×10^{-9} m).

The energy increase is:

a Wave representation	**b** Particle representation

wavelength l

$m = 0$
$E = hf$

● **Figure 3.4** Two ways of thinking about electromagnetic (EM) radiation are necessary in different circumstances.
a In the wave representation, we consider EM radiation as a wave with wavelength λ and frequency f.
b In the particle representation, we consider EM radiation to consist of photons. A photon is a 'particle' or packet of EM radiation having zero mass and energy hf.

$$\Delta E = hf$$

$$= \frac{hc}{\lambda}$$

$$= \frac{6.63 \times 10^{-34} \, \text{J s} \times 3.00 \times 10^{8} \, \text{m s}^{-1}}{120 \times 10^{-9} \, \text{m}}$$

$$= 1.66 \times 10^{-18} \, \text{J per molecule}$$

To convert this value to kilojoules per mole, multiply by the Avogadro constant and divide by 1000:

$$\frac{1.66 \times 10^{-18} \, \text{J} \times 6.02 \times 10^{23} \, \text{mol}^{-1}}{1000} = 999 \, \text{kJ mol}^{-1}$$

SAQ 3.1

Blue light has a wavelength of 450 nm.
What is its corresponding frequency?

SAQ 3.2

Calculate, in kilojoules per mole, the energy increase of a molecule that has absorbed radiation of wavelength 200 nm.

Spectroscopy

There are two types of spectroscopy that use electromagnetic radiation. These are **absorption spectroscopy** and **emission spectroscopy**.

Absorption spectroscopy

When a beam of radiation is passed through a sample, some of the radiation may be absorbed by the sample. This can only happen when the energy of the photons in the beam of radiation exactly matches the energy difference between the ground state (i.e. the lowest energy state) and one of the higher energy states of the atoms or molecules. The energy of these photons is transferred to the atoms and molecules and the beam of radiation is weakened. (You will read more about absorption spectroscopy in chapter 4.)

Emission spectroscopy

When the sample itself is the source of radiation, the atoms and molecules are in an excited state. They drop from a higher to a lower state of energy and emit the excess energy as photons of radiation. The frequency of the emitted radiation corresponds to the difference in energy between the higher and lower states (figure 3.5).

Absorption and emission spectroscopy are concerned with the same energy level jumps (figure 3.6). However, a wide range of radiation is used in absorption spectroscopy, while in emission spectroscopy visible and ultraviolet radiation are mainly used.

Atomic spectra

Atomic spectra are obtained from the gaseous atoms of elements. Atomic emission spectra have been particularly useful in determining atomic structures and in the study of electron energy levels and the Periodic Table.

In *Chemistry 1*, chapter 1, you saw that Niels Bohr proposed a new model of the atom (1913). We find this model useful in understanding atomic spectra. It is referred to as the 'Bohr' atom. At the time of Bohr's investigations, the accepted model of the atom, proposed by Rutherford in 1911, was a positively charged nucleus containing most of the mass of the atom surrounded by negatively charged electrons. Bohr examined the atomic emission spectrum of the simplest element, hydrogen, and as a result of his studies our concept of atomic structure was changed.

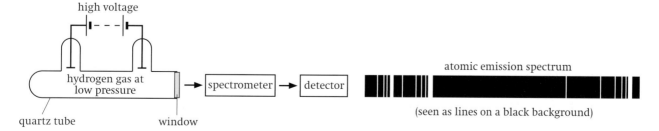

● **Figure 3.5** How the emission spectrum of hydrogen is obtained.

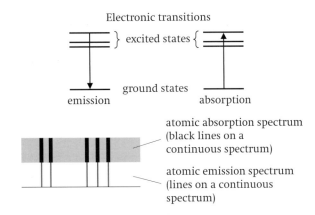

● **Figure 3.6** Absorption and emission spectra involve the same energy jumps and the lines on the spectra correspond exactly with each other.

The atomic emission spectrum of hydrogen

Production of the spectrum

Look at *figure 3.5* again to see how the hydrogen emission spectrum is produced.

■ An electrical discharge is passed through the sample. Hydrogen is already a gas, but liquid or solid samples would be vaporised by the electric arc or spark in the discharge tube.

■ The electrons in the discharge tube bombard the hydrogen molecules, which dissociate into atoms.

■ The electrical discharge also excites the atoms because the electrons in the atoms absorb energy.

■ The excited atoms quickly lose this energy and radiation is emitted. A pink glow is seen because some visible radiation is emitted along with infrared and ultraviolet radiation.

■ The emitted radiation is passed through a spectrometer, where it is split into its different components to produce the spectral lines on the detector.

Interpretation of the spectrum

Bohr claimed that the atomic hydrogen spectrum could only be explained by extending the current model of the atom so that electrons exist only in certain energy levels where they are stable (i.e. do not emit radiation).

The spectrum is formed in the following way. Normally, the electron in a hydrogen atom would be in the lowest energy level. When the electrical discharge is applied, the electron absorbs some

energy and is therefore excited to a higher energy level. The excited electron almost instantaneously drops back to a lower energy level (*figure 3.7*), and energy is emitted as radiation.

Each line in the spectrum is produced by photons of a single frequency and corresponds to a particular transition between energy levels. Bohr also proposed that the frequency f of the radiation emitted is related directly to the difference in energy, ΔE, between the levels by Planck's equation:

$$\Delta E = hf$$

Quantum levels and series of lines in the spectrum.

The electrons in the different hydrogen atoms are not all excited to the same energy level by the electrical discharge. They are spread over a number of levels with $n = 2, 3, 4$, etc. (The symbol n is known as the principal quantum number, see *Chemistry 1*, chapter 1.) Look at *figure 3.8* and see how we can match up electronic energy levels with lines on the hydrogen emission spectrum. When the excited electron in the hydrogen atom drops from a higher energy level, say $n = 2$ or $n = 3$, to the lowest energy level, $n = 1$, the energy emitted produces a line in the ultraviolet region of the spectrum. The electron in a hydrogen atom can drop from any higher energy level back to the $n = 1$ state. The energy, and hence the frequency, of the radiation emitted in each case depends on the difference in energy between the two energy levels involved. Thus a series of lines is formed in the ultraviolet region by the electrons that fall back to the $n = 1$ energy level. This series of lines is known as the Lyman series.

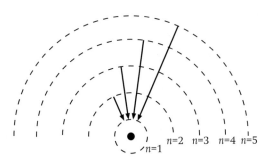

● **Figure 3.7** Electrons in an atom can exist in quantum levels $n = 1$, $n = 2$, etc. Some emission lines arise due to particular transitions caused by electrons falling back to $n = 1$ from higher levels.

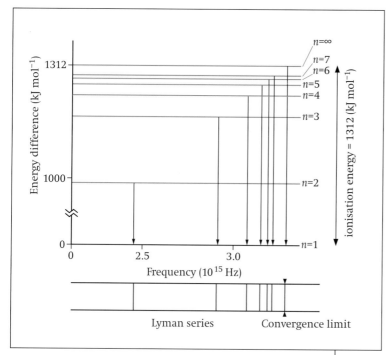

- **Figure 3.8** The energy level diagram for the hydrogen atom is linked to the atomic hydrogen emission spectrum. The Lyman series of lines is formed by electrons dropping from higher levels into the $n = 1$ level.

SAQ 3.3

How does Bohr's model of the atom differ from that of Rutherford?

SAQ 3.4

Why was the spectrum of atomic hydrogen chosen for the study of atomic electronic structures?

The convergence limit and ionisation energies

Look at the Lyman series of spectral lines in *figure 3.8*. The successive lines in the series come closer together and converge towards a limit. Beyond this limit, the spectrum is continuous, no longer showing discrete lines. (From *figure 3.6* you can see that the convergence limits for emission and absorption spectra will be the same). At the convergence limit, the electron that caused the

spectral line has been excited to such a high energy that it is now free of the influence of the positively charged nucleus. The atom has become ionised, that is

$$H(g) \rightarrow H^+(g) + e^-$$

The **first ionisation energy** of an element is defined as the amount of energy needed to remove one electron in the ground state from each atom in one mole of gaseous atoms of an element. In the case of hydrogen this is the energy required to move one electron from $n = 1$ (the ground state) to just beyond the highest energy level in each atom. So the frequency of the convergence limit for the Lyman series of hydrogen must correspond to the ionisation energy of hydrogen. This frequency is 3.29×10^{15} Hz. Using the equation

$$\Delta E = hf$$

we can calculate the ionisation energy of hydrogen (the Planck constant, $h = 6.63 \times 10^{-34}$ J s):

$$\Delta E = 6.63 \times 10^{-34} \text{ J s} \times 3.29 \times 10^{15} \text{ s}^{-1}$$
$$= 2.18 \times 10^{-18} \text{ J}$$

for one electron removed from one atom.

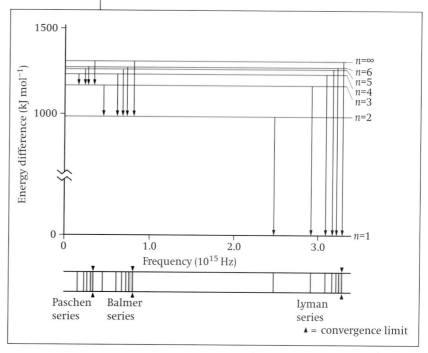

- **Figure 3.9** The other series of lines in the hydrogen emission spectrum are formed by electrons dropping from higher levels into the $n = 2$, $n = 3$, etc. levels

Lower energy level	Region of spectrum	Series*	Frequency range (10^{15} Hz)
$n = 1$	ultraviolet	Lyman	2.5–3.2
$n = 2$	visible	Balmer	0.45–0.79
$n = 3$	infrared	Paschen	0.16–0.31
$n = 4$	infrared	Brackett	0.074–0.11
$n = 5$	infrared	Pfund	0.041

* The series were named after the scientists who investigated them.

- **Table 3.1** Lines in the atomic emission spectrum of hydrogen.

Using the Avogadro constant ($6.02 \times 10^{23}\,\text{mol}^{-1}$), the ionisation energy for each mole of atoms can be calculated:

$$\Delta E = 2.18 \times 10^{-18}\,\text{J} \times 6.02 \times 10^{23}\,\text{mol}^{-1}$$
$$= 1\,312\,000\,\text{J}\,\text{mol}^{-1}$$
$$= 1312\,\text{kJ}\,\text{mol}^{-1}$$

Ionisation energies always refer to the removal of an electron from an atom in the gaseous state after the atom has absorbed energy. The emission spectrum for hydrogen contains other series of lines in other parts of the electromagnetic spectrum. These correspond to electrons dropping back to other energy levels ($n = 2$, $n = 3$, etc.). Details are given in *figure 3.9* and *table 3.1*.

Atomic spectra and the Periodic Table

You may have wondered how we arrived at our present form of the Periodic Table. The atomic spectra of a number of elements were studied and were found to contain many more lines than the hydrogen spectrum. Close examination of the spectra with high-resolution spectrometers showed that all energy levels apart from the first ($n = 1$) are divided into subshells. So, in addition to the principal quantum number n (which defines the main energy level or shell), second, third and fourth quantum numbers were introduced to identify the different sublevels in which electrons may be present within the main quantum level (*figure 3.10*). From this, the number and distribution of the electrons in each atomic energy level of the atoms were found and the Periodic Table was built up (see *Chemistry 1*, chapters 1 and 4).

SAQ 3.5

Would the convergence limit of the Balmer series be suitable for determining the ionisation energy of hydrogen? Explain your answer.

SAQ 3.6

Calculate the energy difference between the 3p sub-shell and the 3s subshell in the sodium atom, given that the wavelength of the orange-coloured line in the atomic emission spectrum of sodium is 589 nm.

The element factories in the stars

Now that you are familiar with the range of elements in the Periodic Table you may well ask where did they all come from. It is generally agreed that the original matter of the Universe was hydrogen gas. We also know that the primary energy source in the stars, including the Sun (our nearest star), comes from the fusion of four hydrogen nuclei to form a helium nucleus, with the release of a large amount of energy.

$$4 \times {}^{1}\text{H} \rightarrow \text{He} + \text{energy}$$

This reaction occurs at 10–20 million K.

When the temperature rises to 100–200 million K, three helium nuclei can fuse to form a carbon nucleus:

$$3 \times {}^{4}\text{He} \rightarrow {}^{12}\text{C} + \text{energy}$$

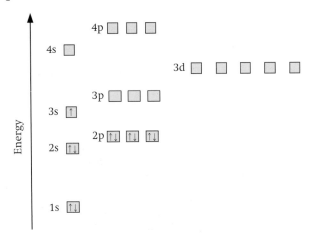

- **Figure 3.10** The distribution of electrons in the sodium atom in the ground state. The numbers 1, 2, 3, 4 represent the successive electron shells; the labels s, p, d represent electron subshells.

and carbon nuclei can combine with more helium to form oxygen:

$$^{12}C + {}^4He \rightarrow {}^{16}O + energy$$

This process can continue until iron is formed, as the heat (energy) generated by one fusion reaction may trigger off the next. Elements heavier than iron are also synthesised in the stars but in this case by the capture of neutrons and the absorption of large amounts of energy.

In the nineteenth century, Robert Bunsen and Gustav Kirchhoff invented spectroscopic analysis following the work of Isaac Newton and Josef von Fraunhofer. This provided astronomers with a valuable tool for studying the Universe. Many elements that were known on Earth were identified in the Sun and the stars by comparing solar and stellar spectra with laboratory spectra. New elements were also detected. Sir Joseph Lockyer identified a line in the spectrum of the Sun, which he believed to come from an unknown element; he called this element helium. This spectrum of the Sun was obtained during the solar eclipse of 1868. The discovery of helium was confirmed when it was obtained on Earth by Sir William Ramsay in 1895, by heating the uranium-containing mineral called cleveite.

Another new element was found in samples of air and identified spectroscopically as argon. From the positions of helium and argon in the Periodic Table it appeared that three more gases should exist. These were isolated by the fractional distillation of liquid argon and were named neon, krypton and xenon.

In 1937 molybdenum that had been irradiated with deuterium nuclei showed traces of an element that filled a gap in the Periodic Table at atomic number 43. In 1952 Paul Merrill detected the lines of this 'missing' element in the spectra of cool red giant stars. This element was named technetium.

Flame emission spectroscopy

In flame emission spectroscopy the samples are vaporised and broken into atoms (i.e. atomised) by a flame at temperatures between 2000 and 3500 K. All elements ionise to some extent in the flame and the electrons of the non-ionised atoms are excited. The sample contained in the flame is a mixture of atoms, ions and electrons. We have seen that Robert Bunsen and Gustav Kirchhoff invented spectroscopic analysis. They atomised samples of elements in Bunsen's burner and analysed the radiation given off by the incandescent vapour with Kirchhoff's spectroscope (*figure 3.11*). They discovered two new elements, rubidium and caesium, and by analysing sunlight showed that certain elements are present in the Sun. This method has been developed to give us the powerful analytical technique of flame emission spectroscopy, which is used for the qualitative and quantitative analysis of elements. *Figure 3.12a* shows a diagram of how the method works.

Flame atomisation of the sample

The process is as follows.

- A solution of the sample is drawn into the apparatus and dispersed into a fine spray.
- The spray is mixed with a fuel and oxidising agent, for example a mixture of ethyne (HC≡CH) and air, which carries it into the flame (*figure 3.12a*).
- The solvent evaporates in the lowest region of the flame and finely divided solid particles are formed.
- The particles then move to the hottest part of the flame, the inner cone (*figure 3.12b*), where

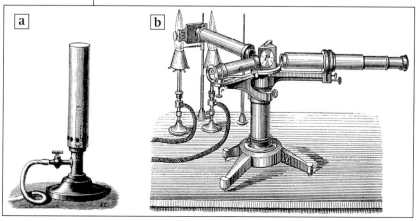

● **Figure 3.11**
a Bunsen's original burner.
b Kirchhoff's early prism spectroscope.

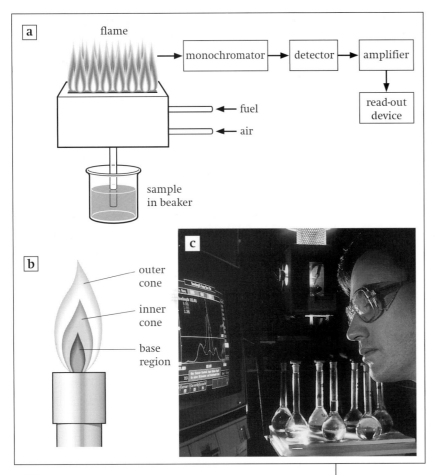

off photons of energy which are recorded as characteristic lines on the spectrum (*figure 3.13*).

■ The intensity of these lines is a measure of the concentration of the atoms in the flame in the excited state.

The 'flame' test

The flame test used in laboratories for the detection of certain metals is a simple, visual way of using emission spectra in analysis. You may be able to try it yourself (see *box 3A*).

SAQ 3.7

Some elements or their compounds are so volatile that their atomic spectra may be produced from cold vapour without the need for atomisation in a flame. Name a metal that could be analysed in this way. (Hint: think of an unusual metal.)

● **Figure 3.12**
a Simplified diagram of an atomic emission spectrometer. The monochromator selects radiation of a particular frequency.
b The different regions of a flame.
c Analysing heavy metal contamination of water samples.

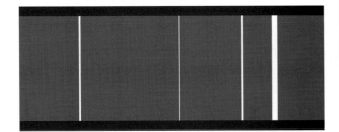

● **Figure 3.13** The atomic emission spectrum of mercury.

(i) gaseous atoms and ions are produced and
(ii) the electrons in the atoms are excited to higher energy levels.

■ The atoms and ions move to the outer edge of the flame, where they may be oxidised before being dispersed into the atmosphere.

■ The electrons that were excited to higher energy levels then drop back to the ground state, giving

Flame temperature in atomic emission spectroscopy

You can see from *figure 3.1* that atoms and ions of the same element have quite different atomic spectra. If the flame temperature is sufficiently high, some of the atoms in the sample will ionise. This ionisation is kept to a minimum by control-

---

Box 3A Carrying out a flame test

■ Moisten a 'nichrome' or platinum wire with concentrated hydrochloric acid (take care not to spill acid on your skin or clothes) and dip it into a powdered sample of the metal compound.

■ Place the wire in a Bunsen burner flame. A characteristic colour is seen with some metals. For example, potassium colours the flame lilac, sodium colours it yellow/orange and calcium colours it red.

This method of detection is restricted to metals with one or two electrons in their outer shell; these can be promoted to higher energy levels by the heat of the gas flame. For most metals, the gas flame is not hot enough to provide the energy for an electron transition, so no characteristic colour is seen.

Gas mixture	Flame temperature (K)
propane/air	1900
ethyne/air	2450
hydrogen/oxygen	2800

● **Table 3.2** Flame temperatures.

ling the temperature of the flame (*table 3.2*).

In general, an increase in flame temperature causes an *increase* in the intensity of the spectral lines. However, when elements that are easily ionised, such as the alkali metals or the alkaline earth metals are heated too strongly the outer electrons move to higher energy levels and leave the atom. These electrons cannot then return to the ground state and so no radiation can be emitted. These metals are analysed with cooler flames.

The extent of the sensitivity of the spectral line intensities to temperature variation is shown in the following example: with a 2450 K flame, the number of sodium atoms in the excited 3p state is increased by about 3% by a 10 K rise in temperature, and the intensity of the emission line also increases by about 3%.

Qualitative analysis

Flame emission spectroscopy is used for qualitative analysis (i.e. finding which atoms are present). Complete spectra are recorded and the elements present are identified by the wavelengths of the lines, which are unique to each element. Comparisons are made with previously recorded spectra from known elements.

Quantitative analysis

Quantitative measurements (i.e. finding how much of a metal is present) are made by using a previously prepared calibration graph and measuring the intensity of a selected emission line. An important application of flame emission spectroscopy is in clinical diagnosis. The concentrations of sodium ions and potassium ions in blood serum and other biological samples are frequently required. For example, a calibration graph is prepared from standard solutions of

sodium ions (*figure 3.14*). The selected wavelength for the emission line is 589 nm. Under carefully controlled conditions there is a straight line relationship between the intensity of the spectral line and the concentration of the sodium ions in the flame in the excited state. The intensity of the emission line at the same wavelength (589 nm) is measured for the sample of blood serum and the corresponding concentration of sodium ions is read directly from the calibration graph.

Instrument manufacturers have designed a simplified spectrometer, called a flame photometer, for the analysis of lithium, sodium and potassium (*figure 3.15*). In this instrument, a low temperature

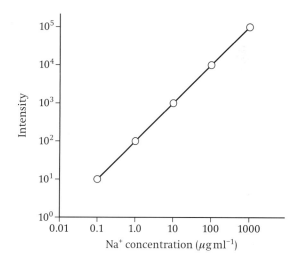

● **Figure 3.14** A calibration graph of emission intensity plotted against the concentration of sodium ions.

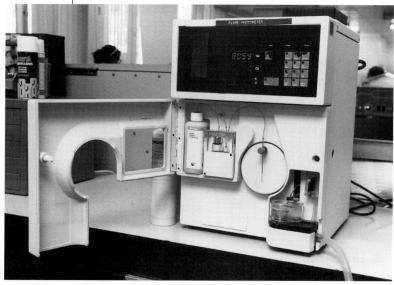

● **Figure 3.15** A flame photometer.

flame is used to prevent the excitation of other metals. The resulting spectra are simple, and the required emission lines are isolated using filters that absorb emission lines from elements that are not being measured.

Flame emission spectroscopy is used for determining the concentration of metals at trace levels. The accuracy of the results is from 1 to 4%. An example of the use of this technique in clinical laboratories is the determination of the concentration of sodium ions in sweat, during investigations of cystic fibrosis.

SAQ 3.8

What are the advantages in using a flame photometer for the quantitative analysis of sodium and potassium?

SUMMARY

◆ Spectroscopic methods of analysis depend on the interaction of electromagnetic radiation with matter. The different regions of the electromagnetic spectrum have different frequency ranges, which have specific applications in the study of atoms and molecules.

◆ The quantum theory applies to all spectroscopic methods. The basis of this theory is that a substance absorbs or emits electromagnetic radiation in whole number multiples of small amounts (quanta) of energy.

◆ There are two types of spectroscopy involving electromagnetic radiation. These are absorption spectroscopy and emission spectroscopy. Atomic spectra consist of lines that are observed mainly in the visible, ultraviolet and X-ray regions. These frequencies of radiation have enough energy to cause electronic transitions.

◆ Atomic spectra were used in the study of electron energy levels and ionisation energies. From the detailed examination of the more complex atomic spectra, the number and distribution of the electrons in each atomic energy level were found. This led to the modern form of the Periodic Table.

◆ Chemical elements are synthesised in the stars. In the nineteenth century flame emission spectroscopy was invented and provided astronomers with a powerful tool for studying the spectra of the stars. This led to the discovery of new elements.

◆ In flame emission spectroscopy samples in solution are atomised in a flame. The atomised sample absorbs energy from the hot flame. Electrons are excited to higher energy levels and then drop back to the ground state, giving off photons of energy which are recorded as characteristic lines on the spectrum.

◆ The intensity of these lines is altered by relatively small temperature changes, so the temperature of the flame must be controlled.

◆ Flame emission spectroscopy is used for qualitative analysis, since complete spectra are recorded. The technique is also used for quantitative analysis. A calibration graph is used to find the relationship between the intensity of a selected line and the concentration of the element.

◆ Flame emission spectroscopy is particularly useful for the analysis of sodium ions and potassium ions in blood serum and other biological samples. A simplified instrument called a flame photometer is used for the routine analysis of these elements. A low-temperature flame is used.

Questions

1   How does atomic emission spectroscopy differ from flame photometry? How does this difference determine the number of metals that may be detected by each method?

2   Using standard solutions of potassium ions and a flame photometer the following data were obtained:

Potassium ion concentration (ppm)	Emission intensity
0.1	4.5
0.3	12.2
0.6	24.0
0.9	30.5
1.2	47.0

From the information in this table find the concentration of potassium (in $mol\,dm^{-3}$) in an unknown solution which gave an emission intensity of 27 (1 ppm = $1\,mg\,dm^{-3}$, K = 39).

CHAPTER 4

Ultraviolet/visible absorption spectroscopy

By the end of this chapter you should be able to:

1 explain that ultraviolet/visible absorption in organic molecules requires electronic transitions between energy levels in *chromophores* which contain a double or triple bond, a delocalised system or a lone pairs of electrons;

2 predict whether a given organic molecule will absorb in the ultraviolet/visible region;

3 explain, in qualitative terms, how increasing conjugation in an organic molecule decreases the gap between energy levels and hence shifts the absorption towards longer wavelength;

4 explain the colour changes in acid–base indicators, such as methyl orange, in terms of a change in the chromophore.

In this chapter we will explore how changes in the electronic structure of ions and molecules caused by the absorption of ultraviolet or visible radiation may be used in the analysis of organic compounds.

Radiation is absorbed by atoms and molecules when the energy of the photons exactly matches the energy difference between the lowest energy state (the ground state) and one of the higher energy states of the atoms or molecules. The wavelengths at which organic molecules absorb radiation depends on how tightly their electrons are bound. The shared electrons in single bonds such as C–H are firmly held and do not easily give absorption spectra. But the electrons in double and triple bonds are more loosely held and so more easily excited. Organic compounds containing these bonds give absorption peaks in the ultraviolet and visible regions. Unshared outer electrons, that is lone pairs that are localised around atoms such as oxygen, nitrogen and the halogens, are also loosely bound and absorb in the same region of the spectrum. (For more information on lone pairs, see *Chemistry 1*, chapter 3.)

Molecular spectra, which are usually absorption spectra, are much more complex than atomic spectra. When radiation is absorbed, the total energy of the molecule is increased. In the diagram of the electromagnetic spectrum (see *figure 3.2*, page 27) we saw how different wavelengths of radiation produce different energy changes in molecules. These energy changes are summarised in *table 4.1*.

All the energy changes shown in *table 4.1* are quantised. Their relative magnitudes are shown in *figure 4.1*, except for radiofrequency, where the differences between the levels would be very small. For the analysis of molecules, methods of

Radiation absorbed	Resulting changes in the molecule
ultraviolet and visible	electronic structure
infrared	vibrational energy
microwave	rotational energy
radiofrequency	orientation of spinning nuclei in a magnetic field

● Table 4.1

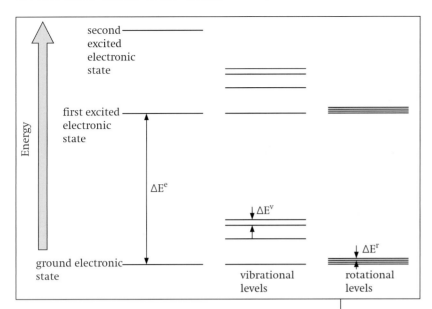

- **Figure 4.1** The relative magnitude of electronic, vibrational and rotational energy levels. This energy level diagram shows the ground electronic state and first and second excited electronic states. Each electronic state is subdivided to show the vibrational levels and each vibrational level has associated rotational levels.

spectroscopy based on three of these absorptions are important as they provide us with valuable techniques for characterising molecules i.e.

- infrared spectroscopy (see *Chemistry 1*, chapter 11, and *Chemistry 2*, chapter 8);
- nuclear magnetic resonance spectroscopy (see *Chemistry 2*, chapter 8);
- ultraviolet/visible spectroscopy (discussed in this chapter).

Production of the electronic spectrum

Ultraviolet radiation from a hydrogen discharge lamp or visible radiation from a tungsten filament lamp are passed through the sample, which is a dilute solution or a gas. The emerging radiation is analysed with a spectrometer to give a **band spectrum**, (so called because, at high resolution, fine lines are revealed within the bands).

Look at *figures 4.2* and *4.3*. These show ultraviolet/visible absorption spectra of two different chemical species. The identity of an unknown substance could be found by comparing its absorption bands with those of known substances. For many molecules, the wavelengths corresponding to the peaks

of maximum absorption have been recorded. However, in general the inferences made would have to be confirmed by other techniques, such as mass spectrometry (see *Chemistry 1*, chapter 1, *Chemistry 2*, chapter 8, and chapter 2 of this book) and nuclear magnetic resonance spectroscopy (see *Chemistry 2*, chapter 8).

Electronic energy changes: ultraviolet and visible radiation
Absorption by organic compounds

Ultraviolet and visible radiation are absorbed by the outermost electrons in organic molecules, which then move from lower to higher energy levels.

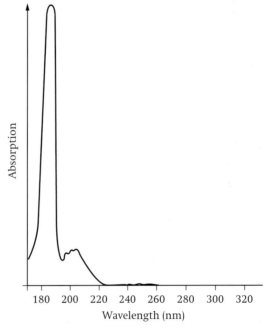

- **Figure 4.2** The ultraviolet absorption spectrum of benzene.

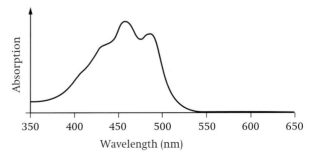

- **Figure 4.3** The absorption spectrum of β-carotene in the visible region.

Two types of electrons are involved in this absorption: *shared electrons* directly involved in bond formation and *unshared outer electrons* that are found, for example, in ammonia:

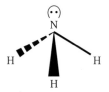

In *Chemistry 1*, chapter 1, you saw how Bohr's simple model of the atom was developed, leading to the idea of **atomic orbitals** (1s, 2s, 2p, 3s, etc.). Then, in *Chemistry 1*, chapters 3 and 10, you saw how the atomic orbitals could overlap to give rise to **molecular orbitals**. A single covalent bond consists of a σ molecular orbital and a double covalent bond consists of a σ and a π molecular orbital (a σ bond and a π bond).

It is the movement of electrons between molecular orbitals that gives rise to ultraviolet/visible spectra.

Colour in organic compounds

Why organic compounds are coloured

You will be aware that although many organic compounds are colourless, some have very distinctive colours. Examples are the yellow aromatic nitro compounds and the strongly coloured large organic molecules that are used as indicators in volumetric analysis.

The colour results from the *absorption* of certain frequencies of radiation in the visible region of the spectrum (i.e. wavelengths between 400 and 750 nm) and the *reflection* (from solids) or *transmission* (through solution) of other wavelengths of visible radiation (*table 4.2*). These absorptions cause electronic transitions between the orbitals within the molecules. All organic compounds absorb radiation to some extent, but most absorb in the ultraviolet region well below 400 nm and so are colourless.

Chromophores

Chromophores are unsaturated groups of atoms in organic compounds that absorb radiation mainly in the ultraviolet and visible regions of the spectrum.

Wavelength absorbed (nm)	Colour observed (transmitted or reflected)
400 (violet)	yellow-greenish
425 (dark blue)	yellow
450 (blue)	orange
490 (blue-green)	red
510 (green)	purple
530 (yellow-green)	violet
550 (yellow)	dark blue
590 (orange)	blue
640 (red)	blue-green
730 (purple)	green

● **Table 4.2** Relationship between wavelength absorbed and colour observed (complementary colour).

The frequencies of radiation absorbed by various chromophores are characteristic of the chromophores and can be used for their identification (*table 4.3*). These values are approximate because:
■ they vary with temperature;
■ they are different in various solvents;
■ they depend on whether there are certain saturated groups, e.g. OH and Cl, nearby;
■ they are also affected by conjugation in molecules (see next section).

Effect of increased conjugation on the absorption bands of chromophores

The wavelengths and the intensities of the absorption bands due to chromophores are altered by *conjugation* in molecules and *delocalisation* of electrons.

Chromophore	λ_{max} (nm)
>C=C	190
>C=O	190 and 280
−C≡N	160
−N$^+$≡N	350
−N$^+$(=O)(O$^-$)	270
⬡	190 and 260

● **Table 4.3** Maximum absorption wavelengths of some chromophores.

A conjugated molecule is one that possesses alternating double and single bonds, for example buta-1, 3-diene, $CH_2=CH-CH=CH_2$. A consequence of this bond arrangement is that the electrons in the π bonds do not remain between adjacent carbon atoms, as they do in isolated double bonds, for example in ethene, $CH_2=CH_2$. Instead, they are spread over all the carbon atoms. They are said to become **delocalised**. You have already met one example of this in benzene, where the electrons are evenly distributed around the ring (*figure 4.4*) (see also *Chemistry 2*, chapter 2).

Where there is conjugation of chromophores in a molecule, the π orbitals of one chromophore interact with those of another and become delocalised. They form new orbitals and the energy gap between the molecular orbitals is reduced (*figure 4.5*). As a consequence of this, the absorption bands due to the conjugated chromophores are shifted to longer wavelengths and their intensity also increases.

Effect of additional chromophores

The conjugation of additional chromophores in a molecule will move the wavelength of the absorption band more and more from the ultraviolet to the visible region of the spectrum (i.e towards longer wavelengths). The diphenylpolyenes

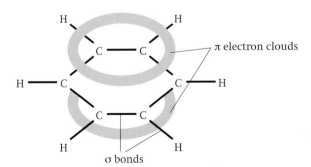

show this 'progression' as the number of –(CH=CH)– groups in the molecule is increased. This is illustrated in *table 4.4*.

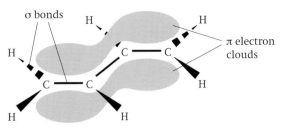

● **Figure 4.4** The structure of benzene, showing the delocalistion of π electrons.

● **Figure 4.5** The conjugation of two >C=C< chromophores in buta-1, 3-diene. The absorption band in ethene ($CH_2=CH_2$) occurs at ~175 nm. In the conjugated molecule $CH_2=CH-CH=CH_2$ the absorption band occurs at ~210 nm, and is more intense.

Dyes and colour changes in acid–base indicators

Dyes are usually large organic molecules that are coloured because they contain chromophores. For example, when a diazonium salt combines with naphthalene-2-ol, a bright red azo dye is formed.

benzene diazonium chloride

+

naphthalene-2-ol

red azo dye

+

HCl

The change in colour in some acid–base indicators may be explained in terms of changes in the structure of the molecules. For example, methyl orange contains a long conjugated system. In alkaline solution this molecule is yellow, but in the presence of excess acid the structure is altered and the colour changes to red. This shows that radiation of longer wavelength is now being absorbed (*figure 4.6*).

Phenolphthalein, another common indicator, is colourless in acid solution, but in the presence of excess alkali the structure changes and the molecule becomes red (*figure 4.7*).

Number of CH=CH groups in $C_6H_5(CH=CH)_nC_6H_5$ (n)	Region of the electronic transition	Colour
1 or 2	ultraviolet	colourless
3	visible	yellow
15	visible	greenish black

● **Table 4.4**

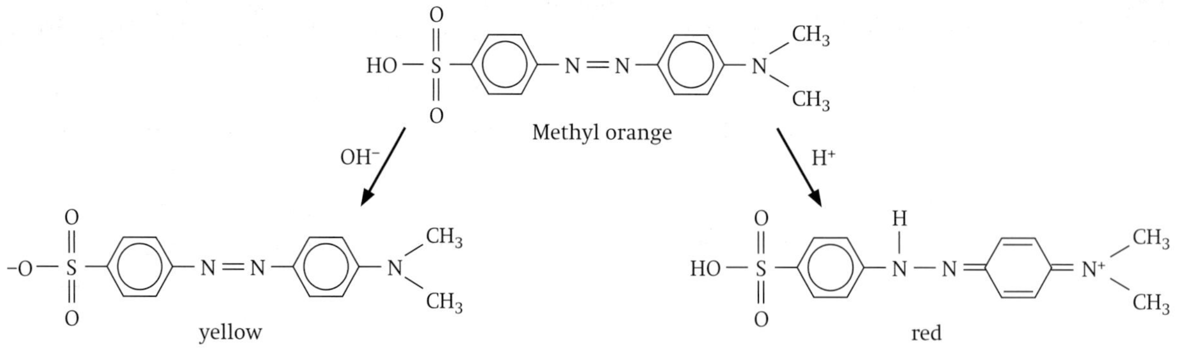

● **Figure 4.6** Methyl orange, showing the changes in structure in the presence of H^+ and OH^-.

SAQ 4.1

Identify the chromophores in the following compounds:

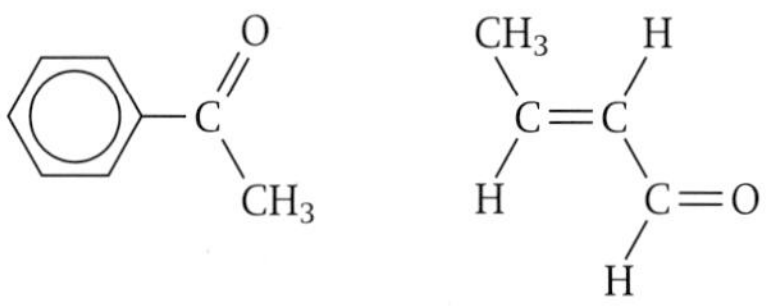

phenylethanone   *trans*-but-2-enal

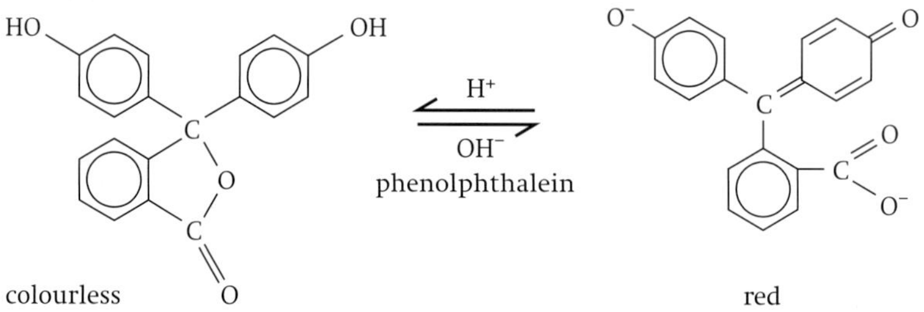

● **Figure 4.7** Phenolphthalein, showing the changes in structure in the presence of H^+ and OH^-.

SUMMARY

◆ Ultraviolet and visible spectroscopy are based on energy changes that occur within molecules and ions when radiation from the ultraviolet and visible regions of the spectrum are absorbed. Organic compounds are studied by ultraviolet and visible spectroscopy.

◆ Molecular spectra contain bands of closely spaced lines, because a molecule absorbs relatively large amounts of energy to give electronic transitions and smaller amounts of energy to cause vibrational and rotational transitions. All these energy changes are quantised.

◆ Absorption of radiation in the visible region of the spectrum causes electronic transitions between molecular orbitals. Reflection (or transmission if in solution) of the remaining wavelengths, in the same region of the spectrum, gives the compounds their colours. Many organic compounds only absorb ultraviolet radiation and so are colourless.

◆ Chromophores are unsaturated groups in organic compounds that absorb radiation mainly in the ultraviolet and visible regions of the spectrum and give rise to electronic transitions; an example of a chromophore is >C=O. The frequencies of the transitions are characteristic of the chemical groups and are used for their identification.

◆ The wavelengths and the intensities of the absorption bands due to chromophores are altered by conjugation in molecules and by the delocalisation of electrons. This is seen in acid−base indicators, when the colour changes on going from alkaline to acidic conditions. This colour change occurs because the structures of the molecules alter and radiation of a different wavelength is absorbed.

Question

1 a Explain how ultraviolet and visible radiation cause electronic transitions in organic compounds.

 b Explain how colour arises in organic compounds.

Combined techniques

The spectroscopic techniques that you studied earlier in this book and in your earlier studies in Chemistry are each limited in the type and amount of analytical data that they can provide.

In this chapter, we will explore how a combination of techniques (infrared, nuclear magnetic resonance spectroscopy and mass spectrometry) enables us to find the structure of organic compounds. With the exception of mass spectrometry, these methods are non-destructive, so the spectra can be obtained with a small amount of sample.

Elemental analysis

When possible, the composition by mass of the elements is determined because this added information is helpful in identifying compounds.

■ Carbon, hydrogen, nitrogen and sulphur can all

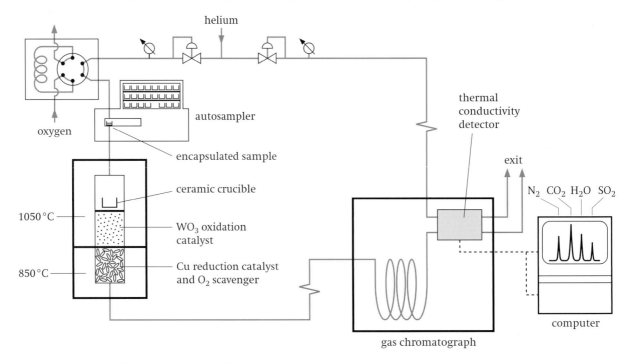

● **Figure 5.1** Schematic diagram of an elemental analyser.

be determined in a single operation by an elemental analyser (*figure 5.1*). The sample is burned in oxygen and the gases formed (CO_2, H_2O, N_2 and SO_2) are separated by gas chromatography (chapter 1) and measured by thermal conductivity (*figure 5.2*).

- Oxygen is determined separately by thermally decomposing the sample in the absence of added oxygen (this is called pyrolysis). The oxygen in the compound is measured as carbon monoxide.
- Halogens are measured as HX.

Identification and structure determination

The contribution that each type of spectrum can make to our knowledge of a compound can be summarised as follows.

Mass spectrometry (see chapter 2 of this book, *Chemistry 1*, chapter 2, and *Chemistry 2*, chapter 8)

- Accurate molecular mass from the molecular-ion peak.
- Possible structure from the fragmentation pattern.
- The number of carbon atoms present from the M and $[M + 1]$ molecular-ion peaks.
- The presence of chlorine and bromine from $[M + 2]$ and $[M + 4]$ molecular-ion peaks (if present).

Infrared (see *table 5.1*, *Chemistry 1*, chapter 11, and *Chemistry 2*, chapter 8)

- The presence of functional groups from the wavenumbers of the absorption bands found in the region between $1500\,cm^{-1}$ and $3500\,cm^{-1}$.
- The identity of the compound using the 'finger-print' region ($700–1500\,cm^{-1}$), by comparison with spectra of known compounds.

Nuclear magnetic resonance (see *table 5.2* and *Chemistry 2*, chapter 8)

- The identity of chemical groups containing protons from chemical shift.
- The arrangement of proton-containing groups in the molecule from the spin–spin splitting pattern.

It is not always necessary to record and interpret all three spectra to identify and to suggest a structure for an unknown compound.

In infrared spectra the O–H stretching absorption bands are broad because of hydrogen bonding. They will only appear as sharp peaks if the sample is in dilute solution or in the vapour phase.

Bond	Location	Wavenumber (cm^{-1})
C–O	alcohols, esters	1000–1300
C=O	aldehydes, ketones, carboxylic acids, esters	1680–1750
O–H	hydrogen bonded in carboxylic acids	2500–3300 (broad)
C–H	alkanes, alkenes, arenes	2840–3095
N–H	primary amines	3100–3500
O–H	hydrogen bonded in alcohols, phenols	3230–3550
O–H	free	3580–3670

● **Table 5.1** Characteristic ranges for infrared absorption due to stretching vibrations in organic molecules.

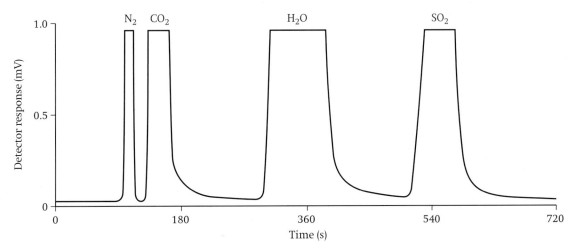

● **Figure 5.2** A gas chromatographic trace from an elemental analyser, showing the separation of the combustion products. Each component is measured under such conditions that the area of each peak is proportional to the mass of each product.

Type of proton	Chemical shift, δ (ppm)
$R-CH_3$	0.7–1.6
$R-CH_2-R$	1.2–1.4
R_3CH	1.6–2.0
$-\overset{\overset{\displaystyle O}{\|}}{C}-CH_3$ $-\overset{\overset{\displaystyle O}{\|}}{C}-CH_2-R$	2.0–2.9
⬡$-CH_3$ ⬡$-CH_2-R$	2.3–2.7
$-O-CH_3$ $-O-CH_2-R$	3.3–4.3
$R-OH$	3.5–5.5*
⬡$-OH$	6.5–7.0
⬡$-H$	7.1–7.7
$R-\overset{\overset{\displaystyle O}{\|}}{C}-H$ ⬡$-\overset{\overset{\displaystyle O}{\|}}{C}-H$	9.5–10*
$-\overset{\overset{\displaystyle O}{\|}}{C}-OH$	11.0–11.7*

● **Table 5.2** Typical proton chemical shift values (δ) relative to TMS = 0. (Those marked * are sensitive to solvents, substituents and concentration.)

Worked examples

Compound A *(figure 5.3 opposite)*
The i.r. spectrum indicates that the compound is relatively simple. The sharp absorption band at ~3000 cm^{-1} indicates a C–H bond.

The n.m.r. spectrum suggests the presence of a –CH$_3$ group splitting a –CH$_2$– group into four parts and a –CH$_2$– group splitting a –CH$_3$ group into three parts. This is the typical spectrum of an ethyl group.

The mass spectrum shows an M peak (m/e 108) and an [M + 2] peak (m/e 110), suggesting the presence of a halogen. The M and [M + 2] peaks are in a 1:1 ratio, suggesting that the halogen is bromine (chlorine would give a 3:1 ratio). The [M + 1] peak is approximately 2.2% of the corresponding M peak, indicating that there are two carbon atoms in the

molecule. The M peak in *figure 5.3a* has a relative abundance of 60.4% and the [M + 1] peak has a relative abundance of 1.3%:

$$\frac{\text{relative abundance of [M + 1] peak}}{\text{relative abundance of M peak}} = \frac{1.3\%}{60.4\%} \times 100$$
$$= 2.2\%$$

The peaks at m/e 79 and 81 (in a 1:1 ratio) show the presence of the two isotopes of bromine (^{79}Br and ^{81}Br). The peak at m/e 29 corresponds to [C$_2$H$_5$]$^+$.

The compound is bromoethane:

$$H-\overset{\overset{\displaystyle H}{\|}}{\underset{\underset{\displaystyle H}{\|}}{C}}-\overset{\overset{\displaystyle H}{\|}}{\underset{\underset{\displaystyle H}{\|}}{C}}-Br$$

Compound B *(figure 5.4 page 48)*
The i.r. spectrum shows an absorption band at ~1700 cm^{-1}, which indicates the presence of a C=O bond. The broad band at 2500 to 3300 cm^{-1} indicates the presence of an –OH group in a carboxylic acid.

The composition by mass of the elements is useful at this stage. You saw in *Chemistry 1*, chapter 2, how the empirical formula of a compound is calculated from this information. The empirical formula is worked out in *table 5.3*.

The empirical formula is therefore C$_4$H$_4$O, and the empirical molecular mass is M_r = 68.

The mass spectrum shows that M = 136. Therefore, the molecular formula is C$_8$H$_8$O$_2$. This is a highly unsaturated molecule (the saturated hydrocarbon with eight carbon atoms is C$_8$H$_{18}$), which suggests the presence of a benzene ring.

Molecules that could fit this data are

or one of the forms of

(i.e. 1,2–, 1,3– or 1,4–)

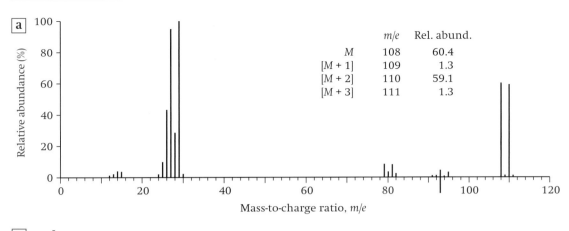

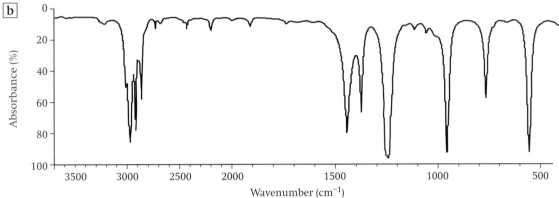

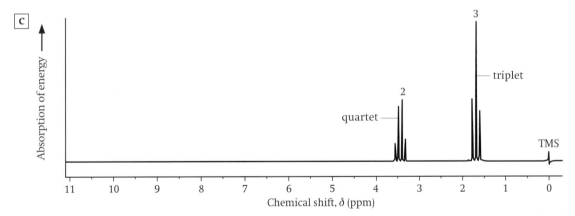

● **Figure 5.3** Compound A:
a the mass spectrum
b the i.r. spectrum
c the n.m.r. spectrum (in CDCl₃).

	C	**H**	**O**
Percentage by mass	70.7	6.0	23.3
Amount (mol)	$\dfrac{70.7}{12} = 5.89$	$\dfrac{6.0}{1} = 6$	$\dfrac{23.3}{16} = 1.46$
Divide by the smallest number (in this case 1.46) to give whole numbers of atoms per molecule	4	4	1

● **Table 5.3** Working out the empirical formula of B.

The mass spectrum shows a large peak at $m/e = 91$, but this could represent the fragment ions $[C_6H_5CH_2]^+$ or

$$\left[\begin{array}{c} H_3C-\hspace{-6pt}\bigcirc\hspace{-6pt} \end{array} \right]^+$$

The n.m.r. spectrum shows a single peak at $\delta = 7.3$, which indicates a phenyl group, and the single peak at $\delta = 3.7$ suggests the presence of a $-CH_2-$ group.

Neither of these peaks is split, so the proton groups are not adjacent.

If $H_3C-\hspace{-6pt}\bigcirc$ were present in the molecule,

a peak would be expected at $\delta = \sim2.3$.

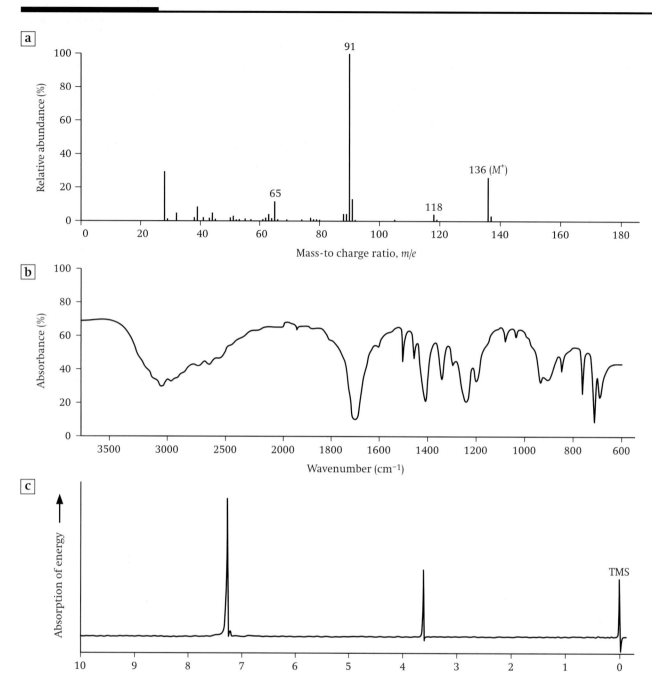

- **Figure 5.4** Compound B:
a the mass spectrum
b the i.r. spectrum
c the n.m.r. spectrum.
Elemental analysis of B gave the following results: C, 70.7%; H, 6.0%; O, 23.3%.

The compound is phenylethanoic acid:

Further confirmation may be obtained by comparing one of the spectra with that obtained from a pure sample of phenylethanoic acid.

Confirmation of a structure

You can see from these examples that, while all the spectra contribute in some way to the analysis of the compound, the evidence from one or two techniques can hold the key to solving the problem. In the analysis of compound A, the mass spectrum made the essential contribution. With compound B, the final choice of structure was based on the evidence from the n.m.r. spectrum.

In many cases, it is important to recognise what further evidence is required to confirm the structure of a compound. For example, in the analysis of a hydrocarbon that has two isomers, the infrared spectrum will only show absorptions due to C–H bonds. The mass spectrum will give the relative molecular mass and the number of carbon atoms, and the fragmentation pattern may indicate the most likely structure. But to confirm a structure, an n.m.r. spectrum would be required.

The use of n.m.r. to confirm the structure of a compound is shown in *figure 5.5*. The n.m.r spectra for the two isomers of C_2H_6O are very different.

■ The spectrum for ethanol (C_2H_5OH) shows a –CH_2– group split into 4 peaks (in a 1:3:3:1 ratio) by a –CH_3 group. It also shows a –CH_3 group split into 3 peaks (in a 1:2:1 ratio) by a –CH_2– group. A peak is also shown for the –OH group (see *table 5.2* for some explanation).

■ The n.m.r. spectrum for methoxymethane (CH_3OCH_3, an ether) shows just one peak as all the protons are in the same chemical environment.

SAQ 5.1

Suggest, with reasons, which spectroscopic techniques would be essential to identify and find the structures of the following compounds.

a $CH_3CHClCH_3$

b $CH_3CH_2CH_2COOH$

c CH_3COOCH_3

d HO—⟨ ⟩—C$\overset{O}{\underset{H}{\lessgtr}}$

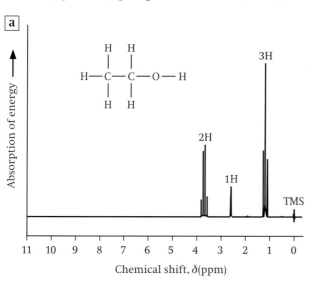

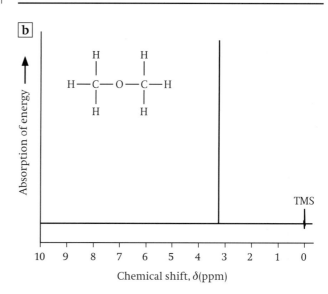

● **Figure 5.5** Structures and n.m.r. spectra of the two isomers of C_2H_6O:
a ethanol (C_2H_5OH)
b methoxymethane (CH_3OCH_3).

SUMMARY

◆ Infrared, nuclear magnetic resonance and mass spectra are all used in the analysis of organic compounds. Frequently, it is not possible to establish an identity or structure from one technique alone.

◆ The compounds are most quickly and easily analysed by combining the three techniques. This is because the information provided by one spectrum may fill the gaps in information from another. The various spectra complement one another.

◆ The method involves recognising the important features of each spectrum and fitting the information together like the pieces of a jigsaw puzzle.

Questions

The following sets of spectra for different types of compounds are provided for you to gain experience of analysis by combined spectroscopic techniques.

1 Identify compound P from the spectra in *figure 5.6*.

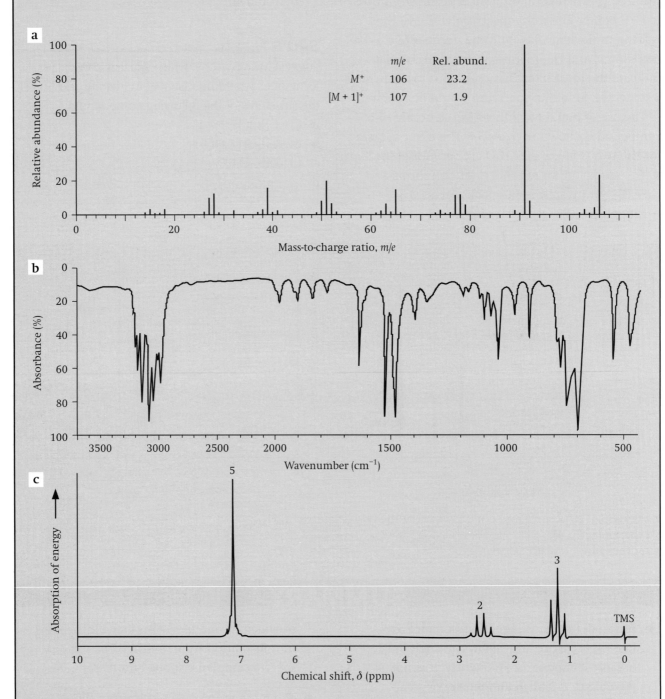

	m/e	Rel. abund.
M^+	106	23.2
$[M + 1]^+$	107	1.9

● **Figure 5.6** Compound P:
a the mass spectrum;
b the i.r. spectrum;
c the n.m.r. spectrum.

2 Identify compound Q from the spectra in *figure 5.7*.

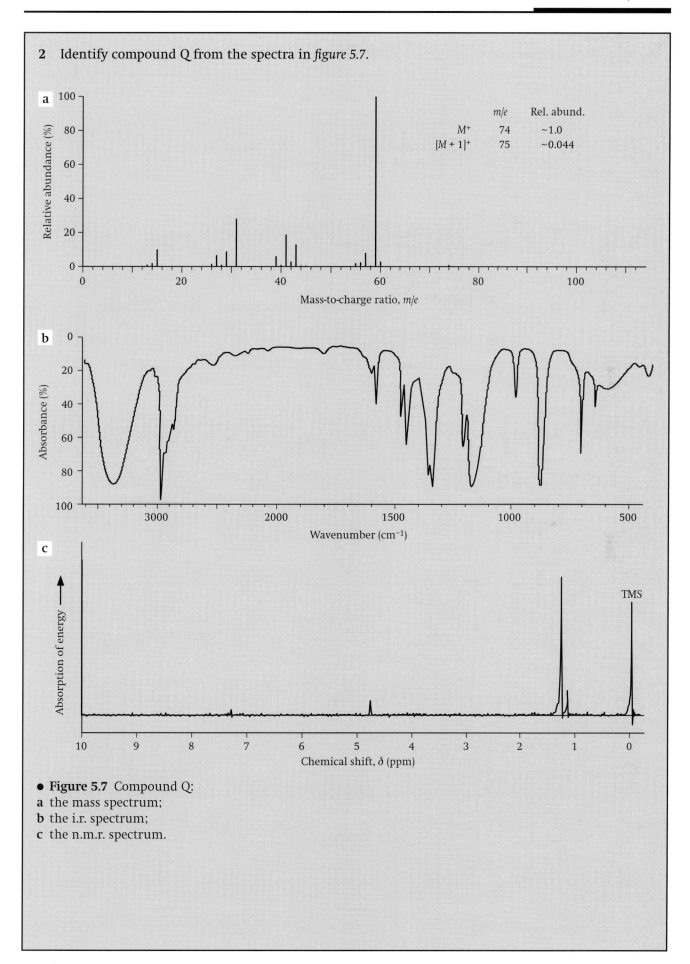

	m/e	Rel. abund.
M⁺	74	~1.0
[M + 1]⁺	75	~0.044

● **Figure 5.7** Compound Q:
a the mass spectrum;
b the i.r. spectrum;
c the n.m.r. spectrum.

3 Identify compound R from the spectra in *figure 5.8*

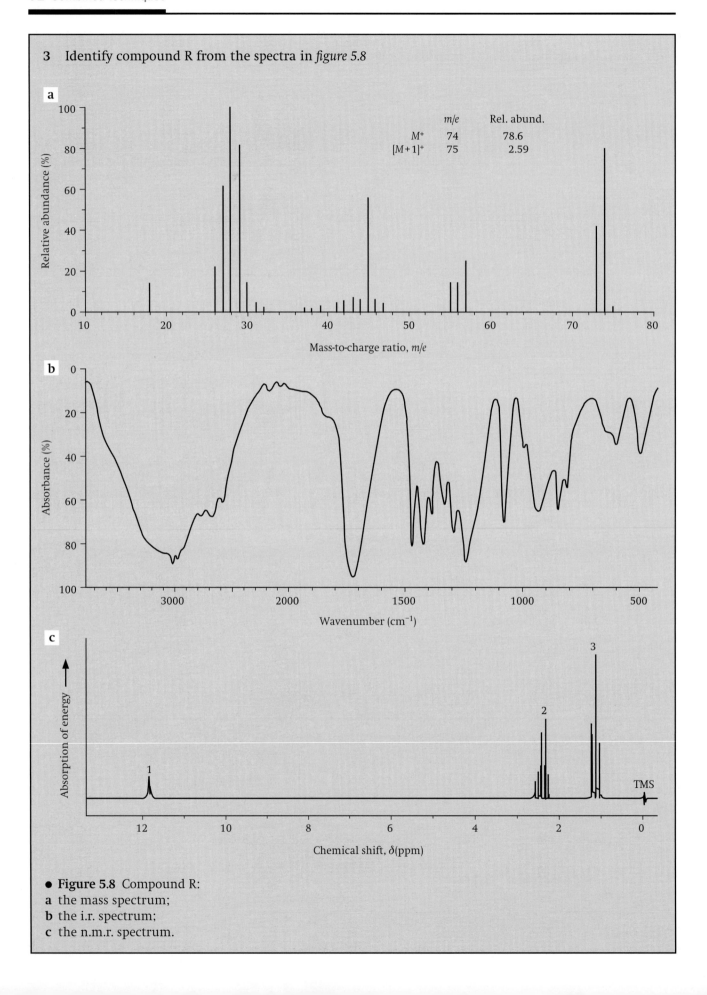

	m/e	Rel. abund.
M^+	74	78.6
$[M+1]^+$	75	2.59

● **Figure 5.8** Compound R:
a the mass spectrum;
b the i.r. spectrum;
c the n.m.r. spectrum.

4 Identify compound S from the spectra in *figure 5.9.*

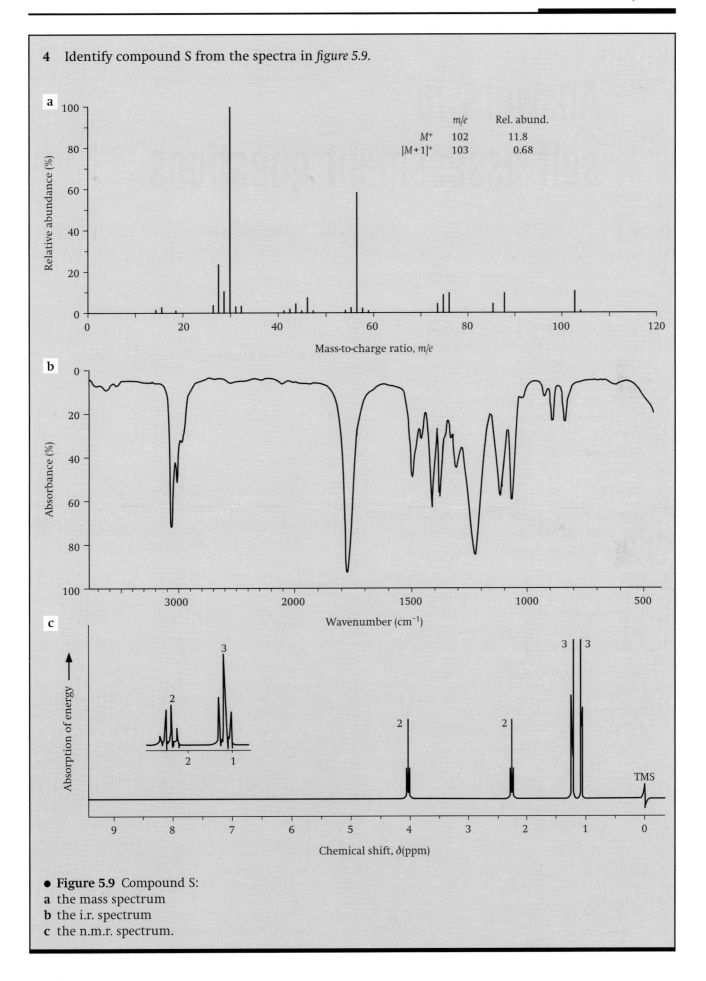

	m/e	Rel. abund.
M^+	102	11.8
$[M+1]^+$	103	0.68

● **Figure 5.9** Compound S:
a the mass spectrum
b the i.r. spectrum
c the n.m.r. spectrum.

Answers to self-assessment questions

Chapter 1

1.1 Any two of the following:
(i) Thin-layer chromatography is faster than paper chromatography.
(ii) The thin layer may be made from different solids. So a wide variety of mixtures can be separated by careful choice of the mobile and stationary phases.
(iii) Thin-layer chromatography can be used for quickly selecting the best conditions for larger-scale separations.

1.2 Compound 1 $\quad R_f = \dfrac{1.5}{12.5} = 0.12$

Compound 2 $\quad R_f = \dfrac{9.1}{12.5} = 0.73$

Compound 1 has a greater affinity for the thin layer than compound 2. As the thin layer is silica gel, compound 1 is more polar than compound 2.

1.3 a By measuring the difference in time between the injection of the sample and the centre of the peak for a component.
b The areas under the peaks represent the amounts of the components in the mixture.

1.4 a Paper chromatography or thin-layer chromatography.
b Gas/liquid chromatography.
c High-performance liquid chromatography or thin-layer chromatography.

1.5 a A methanol CH_3OH
B ethanol C_2H_5OH
C butan-1-ol $CH_3CH_2CH_2CH_2OH$
D 2-methylbutan-1-ol

$$CH_2 - CH_2 - \underset{\underset{\displaystyle OH}{|}}{\overset{\overset{\displaystyle CH_3}{|}}{C}} - CH_2$$

b

Peaks	A	B	C	D
% of total	6.7	66.7	13.3	13.3

1.6 Charge, size and temperature.

1.7 a

$$H_3\overset{+}{N} - \underset{\underset{\displaystyle H}{|}}{\overset{\overset{\displaystyle CH(CH_3)_2}{|}}{C}} - COO^-$$

b The COO^- group becomes protonated.

$$H_3\overset{+}{N} - \underset{\underset{\displaystyle H}{|}}{\overset{\overset{\displaystyle CH(CH_3)_2}{|}}{C}} - COO^- \; + \; H^+ \; \longrightarrow \; H_3\overset{+}{N} - \underset{\underset{\displaystyle H}{|}}{\overset{\overset{\displaystyle CH(CH_3)_2}{|}}{C}} - COOH$$

1.8 Electrophoresis is used to separate the small fragments of DNA on a gel. This method separates the fragments according to their charge and size without altering them in any way.

Chapter 2

2.1 42.0468 $H_3C - C \overset{\diagup H}{\underset{\diagdown CH_2}{}}$

44.0261 $H_3C - C \overset{\diagup\diagup O}{\underset{\diagdown H}{}}$

2.2 a

Peak	m/e	Ion
D	58	M^+ $[CH_3CH_2CH_2CH_3]^+$
C	43	fragment $[CH_3CH_2CH_2]^+$
B	29	fragment $[CH_3CH_2]^+$
A	15	fragment $[CH_3]^+$

b For example
$[CH_3CH_2CH_2CH_3]^+ \rightarrow [CH_3CH_2CH_2]^+ + CH_3\cdot$

2.3 When the molecular ion fragments into smaller pieces, the CH_3 group (mass = 15) may be neutral while the larger fragment carries the charge.

2.4 There are two isotopes of chlorine. The three peaks represent three types of Cl_2^+

m/e	%	Ratio	Ion
70	56	9	$[^{35}Cl^{35}Cl]^+$
72	37.5	6	$[^{35}Cl^{37}Cl]^+$
74	6.5	1	$[^{37}Cl^{37}Cl]^+$

For every $^{37}Cl^{37}Cl$ molecule there are 6 $^{35}Cl^{37}Cl$ molecules and 9 $^{35}Cl^{35}Cl$ molecules. This means that a sample containing 24 ^{35}Cl atoms would contain 8 ^{37}Cl atoms, a ratio of 1:3.

The relative atomic mass of this sample of chlorine is

$$A_r = \frac{(3 \times 35) + (1 \times 37)}{4} = 35.5$$

2.5 There are two isotopes of bromine: ^{79}Br and ^{81}Br. There are two isotopes of carbon: ^{12}C and ^{13}C. There will be six peaks.

m/e	Ion
172	$[^{12}CH_2\ ^{79}Br\ ^{79}Br]^+$
173	$[^{13}CH_2\ ^{79}Br\ ^{79}Br]^+$
174	$[^{12}CH_2\ ^{79}Br\ ^{81}Br]^+$
175	$[^{13}CH_2\ ^{79}Br\ ^{81}Br]^+$
176	$[^{12}CH_2\ ^{81}Br\ ^{81}Br]^+$
177	$[^{13}CH_2\ ^{81}Br\ ^{81}Br]^+$

2.6
a M^+ $[CH_3CH_2COOH]^+$, $m/e = 74$

b M^+ peak is 36.5 mm high. $[M +1]$ peak is 1.2 mm

$$\frac{\text{height } [M + 1] \text{ peak}}{\text{height } M \text{ peak}} \times 100 = \frac{1.0\,mm}{31.5\,mm} \times 100$$
$$= 3.2\%$$

This is approximately $3 \times 1.1\%$, so the compound has 3 carbon atoms

c m/e 15, $[CH_3]^+$
$[CH_3CH_2COOH]^+$
$\rightarrow [CH_3]^+ + CH_2COOH\cdot$

m/e 29, $[CH_3CH_2]^+$
$[CH_3CH_2COOH]^+$
$\rightarrow [CH_3CH_2]^+ + COOH\cdot$

m/e 45, $[COOH]^+$
$[CH_3CH_2COOH]^+$
$\rightarrow [COOH]^+ + CH_3CH_2\cdot$

m/e 73, $[CH_3CH_2COO]^+$
$[CH_3CH_2COOH]^+$
$\rightarrow [CH_3CH_2COO]^+ + H\cdot$

m/e 75, M^+ with one ^{13}C atom

d

Chapter 3

3.1 $f = \dfrac{c}{\lambda} = \dfrac{3.00 \times 10^8\,ms^{-1}}{450 \times 10^{-9}\,m} = 6.67 \times 10^{14}\,s^{-1}$

3.2 $\Delta E = hf = \dfrac{hc}{\lambda}$

So $\Delta E = \dfrac{6.63 \times 10^{-34}\,Js \times 3.00 \times 10^8\,ms^{-1}}{200 \times 10^{-9}\,m}$
$= 9.945 \times 10^{-19}\,J$ per molecule

or $\Delta E = \dfrac{9.945 \times 10^{-19}\,J \times 6.02 \times 10^{23}\,mol^{-1}}{1000}$
$= 599\,kJ\,mol^{-1}$

3.3 Rutherford proposed that the atom consisted of a positive nucleus containing most of the mass of the atom surrounded by negatively charged electrons.

Bohr proposed that these electrons surrounding the nucleus exist in orbits of certain energy levels where they are stable.

3.4 It has the simplest electronic structure with only one electron.

3.5 No. The Balmer series is formed by electrons falling back to the second energy level $n = 2$, whereas the ionisation energy is the amount of energy required to remove the electron from the ground state, i.e. from $n = 1$ level.

3.6 $\Delta E = hf = \dfrac{hc}{\lambda}$

$= \dfrac{6.63 \times 10^{-34}\,Js \times 3.00 \times 10^8\,ms^{-1}}{589 \times 10^{-9}\,m}$
$= 3.38 \times 10^{-19}\,J$ per atom

3.7 Mercury.

3.8 A lower-temperature flame is used to prevent the excitation of other metals. This gives a simple spectrum, and the required lines from sodium and potassium are isolated by filters.

Chapter 4

4.1 $C_6H_5COCH_3$ C_6H_5, >C=O

       $CH_3CH=CHCHO$ >C=C, >C=O

Chapter 5

5.1   **a** $CH_3CHClCH_3$

    (i) Mass spectrometry to find M_r from the M peak, to detect the presence of the halogen atom from the M and $[M + 2]$ peaks, to find the number of carbon atoms in the molecule from the M and $[M + 1]$ peaks, and to find a possible structure for the molecule from the fragmentation pattern.

    (ii) N.m.r. to identify the chemical groups that contain protons, from their chemical shifts, and to find their arrangement in the molecule from the spin–spin splitting pattern.

   b $CH_3CH_2CH_2COOH$

    (i) Mass spectrometry to find M_r from the M peak, the number of carbon atoms in the molecule and a possible structure for the molecule.

    (ii) I.r. to identify the functional groups C=O and O–H in the acid. Or use n.m.r.

   c CH_3COOCH_3

    (i) Mass spectrometry to find M_r, the number of carbon atoms in the molecule and a possible structure.

    (ii) I.r. to identify the C=O group in the ester. Or use n.m.r.

   d

    (i) Mass spectrometry to find M_r, the number of carbon atoms in the molecule and a possible structure.

    (ii) N.m.r. to identify the chemical groups containing protons and find their arrangement in the molecule.

    (iii) I.r. to identify the functional groups –OH and C=O. Or use n.m.r.

Glossary

adsorption chromatography a **chromatography** method where separation of polar solute molecules is achieved by their being held on the surface of a polar solid **stationary phase**.

absorption spectroscopy an analytical technique in which radiation is absorbed by the sample at particular frequencies. The atoms and molecules move to higher energy levels and absorption bands are seen as black lines on a continuous spectrum.

atomic orbital a region in the space around the nucleus of an atom where there is a high probability (approximately 90%) of locating an electron.

base peak the peak on a mass spectrum that corresponds to the most abundant stable fragment.

buffer solution a solution capable of maintaining a particular pH value when small amounts of acid or base are added to it.

capillary column an open tubular GLC column which has greater length and smaller diameter than a packed GLC column.

chromatography the separation of dissolved substances by their different speeds of movement through or over a separating material.

chromophore an unsaturated group of atoms in an organic molecule that absorb radiation mainly in the ultraviolet and visible regions of the spectrum.

delocalisation when alternating double and single bonds occur in an organic molecule, the electrons in the bonds do not stay between adjacent carbon atoms but spread over all the carbon atoms in that region of the molecule – they are delocalised.

electropherogram the visual representation of the results of **electrophoresis**.

electrophoresis the separation of charged particles by their varying movement in an electric field.

electrostatic analyser two curved electrostatically charged plates which increase the resolution of a mass spectrometer by focussing the ions into a very narrow kinetic energy range.

emission spectroscopy an analytical technique in which the atoms and molecules in the sample are already in an excited state. They drop to lower energy levels and emit radiation of particular frequencies to form a spectrum of lines on a black background.

ionisation energy the amount of energy needed to remove one electron in the ground state from each atom in one mole of atoms of an element in the gaseous state. The first ionisation energy is that for the first electron, the second ionisation energy is that for the second electron, and so on.

isotopes atoms of the same element with different atomic masses.

[M + 1] molecular ion an ion that gives a peak at one mass unit greater than the **molecular ion** peak in mass spectra of compounds that contain carbon. It appears because some of the molecules contain the ^{13}C **isotope** which is present with a **natural abundance** of 1.1% of ^{12}C.

mobile phase the solvent in the **chromatography** process which moves through the column or over the paper. It is either a liquid or a gas.

molecular ion (M^+) the ion formed by the loss of one electron from a complete molecule during mass spectrometry.

molecular orbital when an **atomic orbital** of an atom partially overlaps with an atomic orbital of another atom, a molecular orbital is formed. This overlap creates an area of high electron density known as a covalent bond.

natural abundance the amount of an **isotope** that occurs naturally expressed as a percentage of the total amount of the element.

partition the division of solutes between two phases. For example, in **chromatography** the movement of a solute in a solution is determined by its relative solubility in the **mobile phase** and the **stationary phase**.

photon a **quantum** of radiation represented as a particle with zero mass.

polymerase chain reaction (PCR) a process that copies specific sequences of DNA using the enzyme DNA polymerase.

quantum (*pl.* **quanta**) a small discrete amount or packet of energy. Atoms can only absorb or emit radiation in whole number multiples of quanta.

relative abundance in a mass spectrum, the amount of any fragment of a molecule represented as a percentage of the most abundant stable fragment.

restriction enzyme an enzyme that recognises certain sequences of bases and cuts the DNA in specific places.

retention time (RT) the time taken for a component of a mixture to pass through a GLC column.

short tandem repeat (STR) analysis a new method of DNA profiling or typing in which very short, stable segments of DNA (STRs) are used. A combination of different STRs are extracted from the biological sample and amplified by the **polymerase chain reaction**. The number of repeating sequences within the STRs is found by **electrophoresis**. This gives a profile or pattern of lines. The probability of finding an identical profile from another individual within a population is then calculated.

stationary phase the separating material in **chromatography**, e.g. solid particles packed into a column, water held in the fibres of paper, or viscous liquid coated on to a solid surface.

support an inert material such as paper that carries the **stationary phase** in **chromatography** and the electrolyte solution in **electrophoresis**.

two-way chromatography a technique used in **chromatography** when one solvent fails to separate two or more components of a mixture because their R_f values are almost identical. To achieve separation, the paper is turned through 90° and the experiment is repeated using a different solvent.

zone electrophoresis a type of **electrophoresis** in which the electrolyte solution is retained by an inert porous **support**, for example paper or gel.

zwitterion a dipolar ion that exists in solution carrying both a positive and a negative charge. It can act as an acid or a base.

Index

Terms shown in **bold** also appear in the glossary (see pages 57–8). Pages in *italics* refer to figures.